# In Her Power

A Woman's Guide to
Purpose, Peace and Play

For further information contact the authors as listed on each individual author's biography page.

ISBN# 978-1-4303-0522-4

First Edition

# ACKNOWLEDGEMENTS

We wish to acknowledge all the coaches for their participation in writing, editing and providing feedback to one another. We have special thanks to Rhonda Smith for her leadership to start this project, to keep us on track, on time, and keep us working. Thank you to Kara Asilanis Gridley for her fabulous art work featured on the front cover, entitled, "A Morning Comes." Also thank you to Kara and Tim Elston for layout and design of the front and back cover. Special thanks to all those who reviewed our book, to Patricia Omoqui for her eloquent "In Her Power" poem, and especially to Terri Levine for her encouragement and great introduction. Thank you to Donna Colter for her clever rhymes for each chapter. And finally, thank you to the Coaching Institute where we coaches met and came together to co-create such a wonderful and powerful book.

We hope you enjoy our book!

# CONTENTS

# Section Two: Peace

## Chapter Five
**Why Heal?**

**One Woman's Testimony of Healing, Faith And Freedom**

## Chapter Six
**A Legacy For Your Daughter:  Improving Your Body Image For Your Daughter's Sake**

## Chapter Seven
**Loving Yourself Healthy While Creating Your Own Positive Body Image**

## Chapter Eight
**Celebrating Change:  A Goal Oriented Approach to Accepting Changes in Our Life**

## Section Three: Play

# FOREWORD

Terri Levine, PhD., MCC

If you're a man reading this, don't put it down in horror. If you have a wife or daughter, you owe it to them to read this book. Men often find women a mystery -- you'll find nothing mysterious about them once you finish this book and you'll be glad you read it.

You will learn things in here that you won't learn anywhere else. You'll read about stuff your wife may never tell you. You may be able to save your daughter from growing up and dragging negative baggage along with her on her life journey.

If you are a woman reading this, just keep walking with it to the cashier's desk and buy it. Take it home with you. This book is your new best friend. It is also your daughter's new best friend. I am so proud to know the authors who have contributed their wisdom here. Some of our greatest coaches lay it on the line, sharing very personal stories to illustrate the truth that being a woman entails.

Then having helped you identify what your problems are, they teach you how to solve them.

It is not easy being a woman, but it doesn't have to be that way, and my sincerest wish is that you will do yourself, and your daughters, a favor and take the first step in turning your life around. The secret of the first step is found within these pages.

As a professional Life and Business Coach, I have met many women who would have benefited greatly from this advice. These are woman with low or no self esteem, imprisoned in lives of mediocrity that they feel is all they deserve, whose feelings of inferiority stem from a life time of being told they are not thin enough, pretty enough, tall enough or smart enough… and who pass these unhealthy and untrue belief patterns on to innocent daughters, who grow up to perpetuate the myth.

And then we wonder why we have so many teenage suicides, so many eating disorders, so many mental health problems, and so many wealthy plastic surgeons living off the lie that women are not good enough, never good enough unless they chop a little bit off here and add a little (or a lot) there...

As Elizabeth Stahl says in the opening chapter, "If we had grown up thinking that God was a Woman, then we would see ourselves as women in a very different light. " This is just one of many powerful ideas inside waiting to help you awaken YOUR goddess within.

And if you think that this is a feminist book written by women who wear trousers and sensible shoes, think again. You'll be delighted to read Mark Semple's take on women and relationships with their significant other in chapter two.

You'll also learn the best way to speak to your children, specifically your daughters, to raise them to have healthy self esteems and take their place in the world holding their heads high, secure in the knowledge that they take second place to no-one, and that they are "perfect" just as they are.

You just can't put a price on the gifts of self-esteem and confidence. Of course, you can put a price on a book, and the price of this book is well worth it!

**Terri Levine, PhD., MCC.,**

CEO, Comprehensive Coaching U

Speaker and Best Selling Author of *Work Yourself Happy*

www.coachinstitute.com

# INTRODUCTION

In honor of the feminine presence this dynamic collaboration of sisters and a brother was created to share, affirm and strengthen the spirit and power of a woman. Throughout these chapters, we highlight the importance of our powerful purpose here on earth, a woman's path to peace and our divine right to release, let go and play.

The purpose of this book is to guide you back to yourself so you can be not only the original part of you whom you dearly loved and yet put aside temporarily, but the improved you that has developed over time often unknowingly. You have probably discovered some strengths you had not known before. You may have even shifted your career interests as the world of business evolved around you while you were in spouse and parenting mode.

As you journey through purpose you will intimately explore your inner goddess. You learn the importance of tapping into your true connection with life - the place where true abundance and beauty innately exists. Through this connection, this energy, your goddess is born and grows within you. The awesomeness of your inner goddess takes root and blossoms as you practice self-love, self-care and the nourishing of your soul. Through this unfolding, inner balance is restored and your world becomes a mirror of the richness, restoration and peace within.

You will be led to ponder how your role(s) evolved from centuries ago. How did it evolve? Where did the ideas come from? You will be encouraged to imagine what beliefs impacted your choices and what might your choices have been, for example, if you had been taught that the feminine force was important and powerful.

Then as you may desire a new career or even your first career as a spouse, you will be guided in what it takes to be successful together with your spouse. As women with purpose and powerful intentions grow in numbers, it is of great importance that we are able to share our success with our partners. Maybe you will be successful literally "with" your spouse in a business together or you may both be successful "separately" yet "together" toward your life goals.

As you think about your next stage of life, you may go through a discovery stage where you will want to re-determine what your passions are. Passion is the fire, the juice, the fuel that enlivens our purpose. What do you love to do? What did you love to do as a child? What were you excited about in life before you began the gradually giving up yourself for others, even though joyfully at that time? What steps can you take to re-ignite your passion when people around you may resist the changes that come to them as a result of your new freedom of expression?  The answers to these questions will be found as you read through the book.

As your children are growing up, they may begin to show signs of disrespect as they begin to believe they know more than you.  This is a normal phase as you may remember from your years of growing up.  Your children may be dealing with the pangs of your "newness" causing growth and change for them.  Here you will learn how to change that disrespect into respect again.

As you've moved through the developmental stages of your life, you may have anger about times when change was difficult. You may have regrets as to how you lost your innocence or the attitude of others as you made your life choices.  You may realize you have begun to have negative feelings underlying most of your day to day life choices.  You will learn to heal these feelings so joy can be returned to you.  This feeling of joy is often referred to as a positive vibration.  Vibration attracts events and opportunities to you whether positive or negative.  In this book you will learn how to create the vibration of your choice and heal past hurts and disappointments.  This healing is an essential ingredient to your success from this day forward.

What about your body?  Have you let it go?  Do you love your body, no matter what shape it is?  Have you accepted yourself just as you are, fat or thin, large or small. Your acceptance of yourself has an impact on your daughter and her acceptance of herself. Look through this book to discover how to speak to your daughter regarding her looks and her worth so she can learn to feel good about herself and make healthy choices whether you did or not. Learn simple ways of speaking to your daughter that can make a huge difference in her self-worth and therefore her choices regarding men and marriage.

Once you have accepted yourself just as you are you will discover the chapter that shows you how to make healthy choices regarding eating. Regardless of your size, it is wise to learn healthy eating for the sake of your longevity and serving your purpose in life with energy and vitality. As part of living healthy you will learn how to ask for what you want and get it. You will learn how to create your life so movement is a natural part of it instead of a chore you have to do daily because you must.

As you excitedly move through the book, you will be noticing yourself making many positive changes with ease. Next you will be encouraged to celebrate change and accept the changes. Sometimes you will need to set a goal to accept certain changes. Since change is inevitable throughout life, you will learn various responses to change to raise your awareness of your own responses so you can keep or discard those familiar reactions to change. You will learn a goal oriented approach so change can come smoother and more joyfully and tune into the positive effects of change!

You will learn tips discovering your truly authentic self so you can retrieve the feeling of joy in mid-life. As events occur and disappointments come you may have lost your excitement and joy somewhere along the way. Here you will learn how to bring that back. You will learn what to do to release your self limiting beliefs and free your inner self that is screaming to be released. You will learn how to play and notice your feelings about playing and how to discard the negative feelings about playing and bring back the positive ones. You will learn powerful journaling skills that can set you free. You will learn what to do so you can stand firmly in this real self of yours so people begin to accept and respect the real, authentic you which has been hidden from them previously. You will learn how to play again as an adult.

And finally, you will learn to laugh on demand! You will laugh when you choose to laugh from within. You will have no need of outer influence to cause your laughter. You will have the skill of the art of laughter and can enjoy the healing aspects laughter provides. As you have worked your way through all the phases of womanhood shared in this book, your laughter skills will help you "color your day happy!" at will, elevating your day and increasing your energy level as well.

Go ahead and begin your journey and be in your power as you being to sweep through the pages of **In Her Power** right now today!

## SECTION ONE

# PURPOSE

1  *something one has in mind to get or do: plan; aim; intention.*
2  *the object or end for which a thing is made, done, or used*

## CHAPTER ONE

## Awakening the Goddess Within – The Roots of Your Feminine Power

# Elizabeth Stahl

Elizabeth Stahl B.A., N.H.C., is the creator and facilitator of The Goddess Party, Star of Aphrodite Life Coaching and The Sacred Woman's Circle.

Elizabeth has spent 20 years working with the Goddess archetype and discovering her qualities within all women. As a Life Coach, creator and facilitator of The Goddess Party, Elizabeth has supported hundreds of women seeking to become more empowered. By infusing her clients with the essence of the divine feminine already within them, Elizabeth encourages her clients to discover more of who they are and to honor their inner and outer beauty as magnetic sources of their inherent power. Her work focuses on helping women to live a more fully engaged life, by guiding them towards actualizing their dreams, goals and inner source wellness.

Elizabeth has 16 years of experience in the Natural Health Field specializing in Women's Health and Wellness. She is a graduate of The Institute for Natural Health Consulting (N.H.C.) in Montreal, Quebec, a Certified Massage Therapist (The Goddess Massage), Certified Herbalist and Certified Transformational Breath facilitator.

Elizabeth combines her practice as a Natural Health Consultant, with her Life Coaching Practice, Goddess Parties and Sacred Women's Circles. She is available for private sessions, group work, classes, workshops, and Virtual Goddess Parties.

### Elizabeth Stahl

**Boston, MA • 781-704-8226 • www.MyGoddessParty.com**

Understand
Feminine strength.

Share
Personal power.

Live
Your Goddess

Yourself.

Elizabeth Stahl

## AWAKENING THE GODDESS WITHIN - THE ROOTS OF YOUR FEMININE POWER

Awakening the Goddess Within is an invitation to awaken your feminine source of power. It is about nourishing a woman from the roots of her love, beauty and strength, honoring her personal magic and empowering herself from the inside out.

When you hear the word Goddess, what does it evoke in you? Does your mind take you to ancient stories from Greece, Rome and India? Do you find yourself recalling names like Aphrodite, Kuan Yin, Athena or Kali? Are you reminded of girlfriends or influential women who embody the Goddess essence in the way they live their lives, or do words like empowerment and love, wisdom and courage resound within you? Awakening your inner Goddess is a juicy concept, for not only is it an invitation to step into a more whole and complete part of yourself, it is also a gift we share with others, a gift of balance and beauty that has a positive resonant effect on the whole of humanity. The expression of a woman who sees her life as beautiful, makes the world an ever more bountiful place to live.

When a woman steps into her Goddess self, her hearts grows multi-dimensionally. She is able to encompass more of the world within her loving arms, her sense of self-esteem and self-worth increase dramatically, and her life becomes more abundant and blessed in every way. Awakening the Goddess is a call for women to unveil their authentic feminine source of health, light and emotional wellness - it is a call to step forward as the women they are meant to be. *You* are the Goddess beautiful lady, your personal magic is abundant and your true purpose is unfolding. Everyday and in every way you actualize the spark of the Goddess that dwells within you. See yourself as the Goddess, know yourself as the Goddess and feel her magnificence step into your being.

## THE FEMININE FACE OF GOD

The Goddess is recognized as the feminine aspect of God, she is the Yin to His Yang - entirely equal and entirely opposite. The divine qualities she possesses are within the gentleness of loving care, nurturing and nourishing, emotional tides, cyclic wisdom, physical beauty, intuition and honoring the sacred mysteries of life. The Goddess is the feminine source, she is the moon, she is the womb that births life into existence; she is the queen of the home and hearth, the mother of all things, the fierce protector of children, the emotional barometer of the planet and the sensual lover of life. She encompasses our full spectrum of emotions from anger and rage to gentleness and compassion, she is alive within every living organism; be it human, animal, plant or mineral, for the Goddess is life itself.

If we had grown up thinking that God was a Woman, then we would see ourselves as women in a very different light. The world would be a place where a woman's wisdom was esteemed as the most worthy source of insight and where decisions of importance would rest within the woman's council and her Sacred Women's Circles. If God were recognized as a balance between both the masculine and the feminine, then our emotional expressions would be highly valued as holding divine wisdom, for within a woman's emotional life rests her true power; she is the conscience and moral compass of the planet. From her emotions we gauge what feels right and not quite right in the world around us. Our feminine vitality and expression would be allotted and our true pleasures applauded, for all acts of love and pleasure are her ritual. The presence of the Goddess is within all beings, but as women we are the chosen reflection of her animated nature, we are her voice, her body and her essence.

## FOUNDATIONS

So how do we begin to awaken this presence within us, how do we step into our powerful Goddessy shoes?

As with all strong structures, we begin with the roots, the grounding and the solid foundation we need to stand upon. To build a strong Goddess Temple within you, to lay the foundation for loving your amazing life, you must first look to your primary source of wellness, the source of well-being that comes from your sense of self-worth. Self-worth roots you to your inner power, your uncompromising presence, and your magnetic life force. Take a look at how you feel about your right to exist, about your right to take up space, to have your needs met and to stand for what you want. This is the domain of self-worth, to know you are deserving of the very best that life has to offer, to know you are safe and loved as a daughter of the earth.

## SELF-WORTH

The basic premise of self-worth is to know without any doubt that you are unique in every way. There is no one else on this earth like you, there is only you! One of a kind, one in 6 billion, you are completely and undeniably the only you there is. Your true value and worth as was given to you by God/Goddess at birth. Each of us is born with our own special sets of gifts and challenges; each of us comes to life under our own distinctive star, with our own inimitable timing, and the unique alignment of the planets during the time of our conception and the time of our birth. Everyone has their particular set of parents, sole DNA structure and inherent driving force towards their life's exclusive purpose. Because of this utter uniqueness, you can not compare yourself to anyone else; there is no one else like you, so there is no comparison. This also means there is no one greater than or less than you anywhere, we are all equals in every sense; this is the core essence of your self-worth.


## HERSTORY

For the past few thousand years, women have been short-changed of their pride of place. This has hurt our feminine spirit and planet to a great degree. Once upon a time, when a more matriarchal culture flourished, women were revered for their life giving, nurturing presence, and moreover, the wisdom to mediate and transform the warlike nature within men. They sowed the seeds, planted trees, and kept the home fires burning. When women were more in tune with the cycles of nature, our mother earth was honored as the source of sustenance and life itself. Since our societal balance has tilted towards a more masculine agenda, our planetary cultures and climates have been strongly affected. Nature has begun to unravel. Forests are depleted, food denatured and environmental illness is on the rise. Breast cancer claims the lives of so many mothers; this is a real life metaphor for the polluted environment of our Earth Mother, the care giver and sustainer of life. As the pendulum swings from one side of power to the other, a new awakening is overtaking the planet - the Goddess is emerging, and she is beckoning us to awaken and remember who we truly are. We are being guided and encouraged to reclaim this nurturing aspect of ourselves, to reclaim our precious value as women and our collective place in the health of our selves and our planet.

## HONOR YOUR GODDESS NATURE

As women we tend to minimize our Goddess nature, we compare ourselves to others and judge our bodies harshly. Maybe as young girls we were given mixed messages about our value, or maybe we were compared to others in unfair ways, many of us have learned to take these negative messages along with us throughout our lives. Statements such as: "I'm not skinny/smart/sexy/rich/beautiful/young or pretty enough" have been impressed on women's minds since girlhood. These unhealthy claims all amount to a fundamental lie we repeat to ourselves, a lie that stating, 'we are the opposite of our divine nature', a lie that says "I am not good enough". Dearest Goddess, nothing could be further from the truth, you are good enough in every way, and you are perfect, because you are perfectly your Self. Allow the roots of your self-worth to feed your entire being with nourishing love and sustenance. Understand you are Goddesses, my dear sisters; you are the embodiment of beauty and nature as is each individual flower that grows. As the breath of life itself deems it so, to know your true value is your divine birthright.

## NOURISHING

The way to nourish your self as befits a Goddess is in performing small acts of self-love and self care. In my work with women, a recurring theme is lack of time to do the things that nourishes one's spirit. In a maelstrom of work, home, children, soccer practice, ballet recitals, cooking, and cleaning, women are overextended, and at risk of depleting themselves of essential vital energy. I have seen women break down in tears over the unloved parts of themselves, and have heard their grief reflected in the shadow of their (as yet) unrealized hopes and dreams. I have also watched as women took to heart just how undernourished their spirits have become. Even the most powerful women, who seem to have it all, hold the sadness of those who have lost their connection to their true source of power. Women are naturally giving, and this is a beautiful thing. Women are superb at multitasking, and are often able to accomplish a great deal in the space of one day. But we can all get lost in the fray of giving, accomplishing - stretching ourselves to the limit, and beyond. This scenario, in the extreme, can lead to a loss of a sense of self, health, pleasure and play. This is no life for a Goddess!

The moment has arrived to re-set your priorities; to know without a shadow of a doubt that being a depleted Goddess is not what your life is about. When self-care becomes a priority, you will have that inner abundance, strength and vitality to share with your loved ones; you need the fuel to go the distance! Remember Goddess, you are the source of life, from you all things proceed and to you all things return. A woman who puts self-care in its proper perspective and priority, is a woman on her way to a more fulfilling and empowered life.

## SELF-CARE

What are some of the small pleasures that bring you joy? What are some little things you can work into your day, week or month to energize your spirit? Is getting a massage on your list or taking walks in nature, even if nature means stepping out into your own backyard or neighborhood? Is it settling into a hot bath or lighting a candle at the end of the day? What are the gems that feed your spirit? My favorite techniques for self-care and honoring the Goddess within me are manifest in the small things I do.

**Here are some wonderful suggestions to nurture and nourish the Goddess within you:**

*Make an aromatic cup of tea and sip it from a special and beautiful ceramic cup or go to the herb store and create your own unique and individual blend, give it a name like "The Goddess Blend" and when you sip it be infused with the health and strength of a Goddess.

* Take beauty walks - breathe in the beauty of the sky, flowers, colors and fragrances around you, feel the wind against your face, body and skin. Honor the nature of your nature in nature. Remember beauty is in the eye of the beholder. Breathe it in, drink it in, take it in through your five senses and be nourished.

*Sit by the ocean or under a tree and state your prayers, wishes and dreams to the Universe and imagine it saying back to you – "Your wish is my command" just as the Genie in Aladdin's lamp would do. Use your imagination; create Technicolor visions of what you want to draw into your life.

*Anoint the Goddess you are with love and beauty! Use pure body oils and creams that smell delicious and make you feel beautiful when you caress them on your skin. Breathe in the fragrance and know you are honoring your beauty.

*Eating for beauty - prepare a meal with vibrant and alive foods of different colors, tastes and textures and make it from scratch. Take the time to really taste and chew all the deliciousness of nourishing foods. Read books on foods that heal and incorporate them into your diet.

*Keep a journal, make collages, and play with colorful pens. Creativity is the domain of the Goddess. Keep the inner Goddess playful, exploring the many aspects of her creativity.

*Breathe deeply into your body, for five breaths or ten, connecting your breath with your heart and organs and infusing yourself with a sense of wellness. To breathe fully is to live fully, as the breath is the essence of life. Take time to breathe.

*Spend quality time with girlfriends on a consistent basis; weekly brunches, Goddess Parties, book clubs and Sacred Women's Circles. Share stories, laugh and cry together, be each other's greatest supporters, sounding boards and loyal friends. This is the priceless gift of sisterhood.

*Create a sacred space within your home where you can lay your treasures. A space for favorite photos, crystals, candles, quotes and flowers, a place that is comforting, calming and for your use only. Find a place to contemplate your life and surround yourself with the beauty of the things you love.

*Pick Goddess Cards, Animal Cards, Tarot Cards – these simple acts are daily guides that foster insights and create a framework for a daily ritual that is unique and personal. These cards can be found at spiritual bookstores. Choose symbols and modalities one that appeal to you.  You will always get the perfect card.

These self-care suggestions can take minutes or hours - as you feel the need, play flexibly to give yourself the needed care.  What are some of the small pleasures you can begin to give yourself as a source for your own joy, empowerment and well-being? Make a list, allow your spirit to unfold with your desires, choose a few new things to add to your daily life and watch as you become the Goddess of your own domain.


## BLOSSOMING

As a woman grows, she blossoms and blooms, and discovers more of who she is. She is fed by her pleasures as she weaves through her life's challenges and triumphs. She is on a continuum of growth and awakening, she lives, she learns, she loves, she grows. Calling in the goddess is an act of love, it is a powerful re-connection to the unique spark and essence of woman's divine feminine spirit. The inner Goddess is the embodiment of light, love and beauty that is ever present in her wondrous womanly ways. You are She, beautiful Goddess, from birth to death and everyplace in between. See yourself, know yourself and feel yourself as the Goddess you are takes root. Rising from the ashes, as the Phoenix from the flame, the

Goddess is ready to take her place at the throne of her feminine power. Unlock, unleash, unravel and step into your true calling. You are the Goddess dearest one, of this I am here to remind you.

*TRUTH IS BEAUTY, BEAUTY TRUTH*

*LET THERE BE BEAUTY AND STRENGTH WITHIN YOU*

*Elizabeth Stahl*

*CHAPTER NOTES*

## CHAPTER TWO

## Being Successful Together

# Mark Semple

Mark Semple is the founder of Successful Together Coaching. Mark is a dedicated husband who supports his wife in her business & her life, and truly understands the difference a supportive spouse can make.

As a Direct Sales Support Coach, Mark works with women in home businesses, primarily Direct Selling/Network Marketing, who have yet to gain the support of their significant other.

Mark has been featured in the best-selling book 'More Build It Big' and on www.TheNetworkMarketingMagazine.com.

Mark is available for group & individual coaching, speaking, tele-seminars and workshops.

### Mark Semple

Pendleton, IN • (317) 485-2197 • www.SuccessfulTogetherCoaching.com

For the team approach,
You need a coach
And Mark is just the man.


He takes your vision
and goes to the schism
and supports you through to "We can"!

## BEING SUCCESSFUL TOGETHER

As the journey of a woman's life unfolds, she will undoubtedly realize many successes along the way. For too many women, these successes are private victories that they celebrate either by themselves, or with their closest friends.

More & more women are realizing that their lives are not as fulfilling as they know they could be and are recognizing that they have the power to create the life that they love.

As they embrace this new vision and chart the course to the future that they desire and deserve, many women are noticing the absence of the most important person in their life - their significant other.

In most cases, their spouses are great men overall - they deserve the honor of sharing her life.

It is a fact that a woman does not need a man to be successful in life, in business or any pursuit she sets her focus on. She has all the talents, power & resources to be a great success at anything she desires.

Being able to share your success with the person you share your heart & soul with simply makes the journey so much more fulfilling and can contribute to achieving greater success sooner.

## DEFINING SUCCESS

The term 'success' has different meanings for different people. And, there are as many different definitions of success as there are ways to be successful. The obvious material symbols of success are money, title, bonuses, houses, jewelry and so forth.

Although we are entitled to enjoy the finer things in life, success also has many facets that are not material. For example, happiness, peace of mind, time with loved ones, and health.

As a couple consists of two individual people, it is a given that there will be some different perspective on what success means. And, that is okay. What must be established is what it means to be successful together.

If a couple has all the material success that they could wish for, but are rarely in the same place at the same time, are they truly successful? My personal opinion is an emphatic 'No!'

Being successful together means being able to be together and have the opportunities to enjoy whatever your lifestyle provides for you -together.

## COMMUNICATION

Determining a shared vision of success requires a deep, meaningful level of communication. Of which, the most important skill is listening. Deep listening; truly hearing and connecting with your mate's perspective, dreams, passions & fears. Hearing the meaning behind their words.

Although you may not be able to fully understand why your significant other feels the way they do - you do not need to understand something to respect it.

As Steven Covey says, "It is more important to understand than to be understood. "

This level of communication will provide a solid foundation to build your joint success upon and will ensure that your success journey provides the optimum fulfillment to you both.


## RECOGNIZING DIFFERENCES

No matter how closely you are bonded with your soul-mate, there will be some differences that occur in your lives. These are simply expressions of our uniqueness and must be acknowledged & accepted for just what they are.

It is imperative that you respect your significant other's differences and do not expend time or energy trying to correct them.

23

Instead, look for opportunities to utilize each of your uniqueness to your mutual advantage.

## AGREE TO DISAGREE

To overcome challenges differences present, you simply must agree to disagree. Ahead of time, discuss your options to mitigate disagreements by choosing a method to satisfactorily reconcile any issues.

It is absolutely imperative that you pursue win-win solutions in all instances. Remember, you are striving for success together. You win together or you do not - it's that simple.

If a disagreement cannot be resolved to joint satisfaction, take the opportunity to step back and determine how important is the issue? Is it critical to your shared success of happiness or is it a minor bump in the road of life? It is far more important to be happy than to be 'right'.

## SETTING THE BOUNDARIES

As the framework for your shared success is taking shape, it is important to establish clear, agreed-upon boundaries that you will both honor. Boundaries will enable you to establish what is truly important to your lives and what is non-negotiable. This can include being home together, having meals together, time for fun and ensuring there is always 'us' in 'business'.

If you and your spouse are in different vocations, the potential for differing schedules is significant. This can be minimized by agreeing on the times, dates and events that are your time and are non-negotiable.

## FOCUS ON THE JOURNEY

When you create a clear, compelling vision of your life & success together, you provide the means to choose the right actions and maintain the motivation to keep moving & growing together.

By regularly connecting to your vision you become more empowered and maintain the necessary focus on that which you are committed to transform into your reality.

There will be occasional periods where extra effort & commitment may be required that impacts your time together. Ensuring this is mutually acceptable & agreed upon, for a clear, tangible benefit to your success together will ensure this remains the exception and does not become the rule.

As your journey progresses, and you begin to experience the success you desire & deserve, and have more fulfillment in your lives, your needs & goals may change also.

Just as your perspective on life changes as your life unfolds, your perspective on other aspects of your lives may change also.

Stay close to your vision and treat it as a living thing. Adjust it as you both feel necessary to reflect the changes in your journey together.

## TAKE CARE OF YOURSELF

The most critical component of success together is you. A healthy relationship consists of 2 healthy people. Your success requires your presence.

Both of you must maintain a priority on your physical, emotional & spiritual health so as to optimally contribute to your shared life & success.

As your journey unfolds, it is crucial that you ensure that your self-care is maintained as one of your highest priorities. We know that life does take some unforeseen turns and not everything proceeds according to plan.

Keeping you as your first priority, will minimize the impact of such interruptions and will maximize your ability to take things in your stride.

It will not matter what level of material success you achieve if you do not have your health.

## YOU MAY START SOLO

The vision of shared success and a spouse who shares the journey with you is truly wonderful. Many women turn to entrepreneurship as the means to create the future they see for themselves and their families. Unfortunately, too many of them start out by themselves as their significant other does not share their vision yet.

Although a shared vision is a true blessing, you may have to hold that vision by yourself for a while. Remember that your success is solely contingent upon you. You will achieve whatever it is that you set your heart on.

There are many men out there who, despite being great people & spouses, just don't get what their wives are trying to accomplish and they don't see & appreciate the power that she has.

Your spouse may not believe in your business. Hopefully, they believe in you. Unfortunately, there are exceptions. Too many women have spouses that are blatantly negative towards their ambitions & efforts. No matter how she attempts to present what she is doing and what she is working for, the other half is unable or unwilling to see it.

Being successful together may seem like a distant dream in this scenario. If this describes you, you must recognize that it is your spouse's limitation - not yours.

There are many reasons why some men are this way. A lot of men can't grasp the concept of a home business. Their concept of producing income is rooted in their perception and they simply cannot see anything that does not fit their image. There also men who feel threatened when their wife claims her power and starts to be successful. Although most men would not admit it, many need reassurance that they are secure in their relationship.

Regardless of your spouse's current perspective, the only opinion that truly matters at the outset is yours. You must believe in you. You must know that you are going to achieve what you see in your vision and - you must believe that it is just a matter of time before your spouse appreciates your greatness and joins you in being successful together.

**TO YOUR SUCCESS**

It is a given that there are no limitations on how successful a woman can be. Whatever she dares to dream is what she can achieve.

When she shares the journey with a spouse that believes as she does, the door opens to the best life possible.

*Enjoy your success – together! Mark Semple*

*CHAPTER NOTES*

## CHAPTER THREE

## Passion is Power:  Keep it Alive!

# Juanita Bellavance

Juanita Bellavance is CEO, Co-Founder, Audacious Enterprises™

As an Audacious Marketing Mentor and Business Building Coach, Juanita mentors entrepreneurs and business owners in effective marketing techniques. As people apply these techniques and see results, their passion for what they do surges forward even when discouragement may have been their state of mind before.

As a former teacher of elementary school music, Juanita discovered ways of maintaining enthusiasm and excitement while students mastered complex concepts and thrived in boundless joy throughout the process.

As passion is ignited in adults, we experience a sensation of being ageless. We reconnect with the joy of childhood and the twinkle returns to our eyes. Marketing mastery is one of the key components to igniting or re-igniting excitement and passion in entrepreneurs and business owners.

Juanita's own enthusiasm and passion is contagious.  In the chapter, Passion is Power:  Keep it Alive!  begin to learn her secret and apply it to your own life. Get excited!  Get the twinkle back in your eye!

Email: **Juanita@AudaciousMarketingMastery.com**

### Juanita Bellavance

**Cumming, GA   Juanita@AudaciousMarketingMastery.com**

For passion to find

Cause you left it behind,

Take kind care of self

Build emotional wealth.

Juanita Bellavance

## PASSION IS POWER: KEEP IT ALIVE!

You see the twinkle in your child's eyes. You don't want that twinkle to ever go out, but you know that soon enough, school or life experiences will extinguish it. In this chapter you will discover easy techniques to keep your child's eyes twinkling with that vital passion we all start out with in life.

While these techniques may not be proven in a scientific laboratory of psychologists, they are based on my own observations of my own constant passion, seeing my children having the same degree of passion and seeing the same thing occur with private music students as well as while teaching hundreds of children elementary school music.

For example, as an adult I have wondered why as a child  I pursued activities such as sewing playing my flute and jack stones and games to the point of spending eight hours a day or into the wee hours of the night?   I seemed to never tire of doing what I enjoyed so much.

Why did my private flute students demonstrate the same sort of behavior, having to be almost forced to stop practicing long enough to do other homework – while other music students seem to have to be made to practice even thirty minutes?

And why was the middle school choir filled up to 50% with students feeding in from the school where I taught music when four other schools fed into the same choir?   The students had an exuberance for music which resulted in their success.  What instilled this in them?

As an adult why do groups where I participate seem to get invigorated with the energy of excitement and then grow in numbers and enthusiasm while I am a participant?   As a team leader of a group of six people, why does the entire group of fifty who are affected by an event end up excitedly creating the event together while never feeling like there is "too much to do?"  What is the secret to this?

**Have you noticed your passion and excitement for life has diminished? Are your children gradually losing passion as well?**

In this chapter I will share my observations about passion and enthusiasm to add to your own thoughts and quest for passion in your life if it has diminished as well as assuring your child's passion remains intact throughout life!

We are all born with passion; it is part of being alive. Passion deserves to be nurtured. Keeping it alive in ourselves is the first step to keeping it alive in our children.

Passion is the magic we feel when we are excited about anything. This excitement could be about a piece of artwork, being successful in a particular endeavor, or being in awe at the sight of a newborn baby.

When you feel that magical feeling, do you stifle it by telling yourself it's childish? Do you stuff it away, putting the needs of others before your own? Do time and financial constraints drain the joy out of doing the things you once loved?

It is easy to maintain your passion as a child; children are naturally joyous and curious. But keeping it alive into adulthood, with all the pressure and stress you have to deal with as you get older, is more difficult.

**Let's begin by observing passion in children. Then, we will add ideas for maintaining passion as an adult.**

Imagine a baby's delight the moment he or she discovers the joy of seeing an adult smile. Imagine the delight you as an adult experience when a child's face is lit up by your smile. Bask in that image. Experience the refreshing bliss of such a moment like an oasis in the dry, pragmatic desert of adulthood.

Now, picture the day when the same child discovers the magic of blowing bubbles. The child tries endlessly to "catch" a bubble, squealing with delight as bubbles lightly hit his face.

And then think back to the day your child made the connection between words and objects, suddenly realizing that words communicate a specific expression. The child's enthusiasm and energy was overwhelming, wanting you to constantly name everything around them.

If you showed excitement with your child in a way that has the child highly enthusiastic about many subjects, you may have gradually backed off from the intensity of the matter. Probably before you knew what hit you, being the source for their exuberance may have become overwhelming to some degree so you cut back on your involvement. While this more balanced approach was good for your child so the child could develop a more inner passion, your passion may have begun to die. It's not intentional; we just cannot be under the child's complete control since we have other important responsibilities that will not allow us to simply be there giving our full attention to the child. At the moment of discovering your limited time for your child's unlimited supply of energetic exuberance, you may find yourself wondering where the information was derived that preschool age children have a short attention span.

How you, the parent, handle this moment will affect whether your child's excitement is harnessed powerfully or is killed through discouragement.

What can you do to harness enthusiasm, excitement, and passion in your child's life as well as your own? While the theory I will reveal to you has not been clinically proven, it has been substantiated by my observations of what I believe has impacted the passion of myself, my children, and hundreds of other children I taught in public elementary schools. I noticed the same enthusiasm with high school students at my church. As a leader of an adult team, I watched enthusiasm mount as we shared a creative process.

While the technique you are about to learn can have amazing results for all age groups, it is most effective for people who experienced encouragement between the ages of zero to five. The longer a person has gone without using this technique, the longer it will take to see the results. No matter how old you are, this technique is effective if you have faith in its power.

As with most secrets for success, this one is so simple and obvious, you won't believe you didn't see it sooner. The truth is, you probably did, but didn't realize its power. You may have used it to a lesser degree than you would have had you realized its power and long-term benefits.

**First, let's see how the technique can be applied to your children.**

This technique can simply be called "excitement." Initially it helps, when you engage in an activity with your child, say blowing bubbles, if you exhibit the same exuberance and fascination for bubbles that your child does. Your child may maintain a high level of excitement for months, but once you establish that you share the fascination, your child won't need you to continuously show it. What your child needs from you is consistent access to enjoying the bubbles, which may or may not involve you completely. Others may also wish to blow bubbles with your child and enjoy his or her delight, but it is important that you do it often.

Part of the child's delight is the attention he receives from you at the moment you blow the bubbles. For example, electric bubble blowers hold some fascination for a child, but not the joy associated with the human interaction. The electric bubble blower can assist in a mechanical sense, but can never replace the exuberance your child experiences when you become a "child" as well, watching the bubbles together.

Human interaction and sharing the child's enthusiasm are key factors in keeping your child's passion alive. These practices can be carried into almost every realm of learning. For example, watching educational programs on television can free up energy for parents, as the child learns what might be exhausting for the parent to teach. However, if television is your child's only source of learning, its power will gradually diminish because what is missing is the interactive sharing that strengthens enthusiasm and passion.

Therefore, it is important to watch television with your child and plant the seeds of excitement about what is being viewed. Because emotion increases memory, if all learning is received via the unemotional television "box," the senses gradually become numb.

Human interaction will increase your child's learning far more than with television's limited interaction. As with everything in life, balance is the key - balancing interactive time with television time is ideal.

Another possibility to consider is the impact of consistently, consciously, and deliberately displaying enthusiasm around your children. Maybe you aren't excited about walking to the garbage dump to see where garbage ends up and how it gets there, but you can still encourage your child's eagerness about the subject of garbage. You may see taking the garbage out as a routine chore that holds no particular excitement for you, while your child may be fascinated by this new activity. By showing your enthusiasm even for mundane tasks, you teach your child to be excited, interested, and curious even while performing the simplest activities. Even if a subject holds little interest for you, your excitement is contagious and encourages your child's excitement.

When your child begins school, you can plant seeds of excitement in your child for school work and homework simply by taking an active interest.

**A word of caution:** regarding involvement and interaction: your total involvement in everything your child does can make the child dependent on you for his or her happiness.

It's natural sometimes for you to have less enthusiasm than your child. After all, you are an adult and information that may be novel to your child is no longer new and exciting to you. Again, balance is important in your interaction with children so they recognize your connection and your interest in what they are doing. It is also vital to children's self-esteem and growth that they feel acknowledged and appreciated.

Be involved enough to know your children and be able to relate to the topics that interest them. Do you have to become a musician for your musician child to feel known by you? Not at all.

Do you need to attend performances, band concerts, baseball games, or other activities in which your child participates? Do you need to acknowledge your child's talent and how proud you are of his self-motivation to practice? Absolutely. It would certainly not be encouraging if you did not support your children by being at the events that are important to them.

Just being at an event and making no comment afterwards is almost as discouraging as not being there at all. Eventually your child will want to interact with you about how the event went, which brings us back to the interactive element of encouragement.

Positive interaction with your child is the "secret" to embellishing the child's enthusiasm about life and learning passionately. I have observed this at every age including high school and college. It affects the levels of your child's passion and confidence. You can understand how powerful this information is when you consider the interactive attention you and your spouse need to maintain enthusiasm and passion in your relationship.

If you are not receiving interactive attention readily and consistently from those close to you, your passion will gradually seep away.

**How can you re-ignite your own passion?**

First, you must want passion in your life enough to take action. What have you been passionate about in the past that you miss and want to re-ignite? As an adult, you may need to find an environment that allows your passion to flourish.

To find nourishing activities and people, you might join an organization that shares the purpose that is important to you and excites your passion. For example, if your passion is sewing or quilting, join a quilting organization or take a sewing class. There is an organization for almost any interest where like-minded people gather to share their expertise and joy. It is easy to find such organizations by typing into an internet search engine a key word relating to your passion. When you connect with others with similar interests, you will realize how many people share your passion, where before you seldom met anyone with a similar interest.

If you cannot find an organization or group of people in your geographical area, you might want to form a group yourself. Remember, "You must want it enough to take action upon it." When you first begin to act on your passion, your family may experience a transition in accepting this you who is new to them. When people around you see you doing something different than what they have known you to do for many years, they resist. They will have an adjustment period.

Keep in mind that for you to solidly follow your passion, your children will ultimately be set free to follow their own passions. You are the role model. Even if they seem resistant at first, you are the one who knows the long-term benefit of you being independent enough to find avenues of enjoyment that do not involve your family, while continuing, of course, to maintain a balance of sharing in their joys.

The resistance your family may show in this newly visible part of you is exactly the reason why you will need to put yourself in an environment of other people who are joyful with you in the same passion. Their passion will ignite your passion and vice versa. In essence you are gaining the exuberant support as an adult that was mentioned previously here for you to give to your child. The human interaction of sharing excitement is explosive in nature and can spread like a wildfire to hundreds of others, including your own family sometimes!

Forming a group or organization will take some time and effort, but this can be an enjoyable process. The amount of time it may take is unpredictable, but the effort will produce results. To build interest in your hobby or passion, treat it as if you were building a business. In many ways, what you are creating is a business without the financial concerns. There are specific, yet simple techniques to accelerate your building process. Learn them by listening to the information at **www.yourmarketingfunnel.com.**

Without using these techniques, a business, organization, or hobby organization will not get off the ground.

Remember, just as there is a process for learning and developing your passion, there is a process for nurturing your environment. That process often becomes enmeshed in your passion, as everything about the process is about your passion.

For now, determine what your passion is if you don't already know. Look into your childhood as well as adult activities you have found enjoyable. If you have lost your "self" in your caretaking of others and barely know yourself enough to choose an invigorating passion, you can benefit from the Power Vision Writing Guidebook at **www.audaciousmarketingproducts.com** . I wrote it to help people rediscover their inner passions and determine what they wish to do with the rest of their lives once they are ready.

In today's world it's still valuable for a woman to put her family first. As she nurtures her family and helps them become more independent, she may find herself with more time to fill. Her attitude and level of enthusiasm can make this a discouraging time or an exciting time.

Maybe you have put your personal passions aside to raise your children. Or maybe your children have been your passion. As they get older, they continue to "need" you emotionally, but need less of your time.  It is important at this time in your life to have interests of your own.

Remember the things you loved to do before your children were born, the things you had no time for while you were busy raising them? Now is the time to re-ignite those interests. If you have forgotten what they were or even that you had them at all, use the Power Vision Writing Guidebook and rediscover yourself!

If you know what your interests are, get involved with others who share that interest. To start your own interest group and move forward, follow the information at: **www.powerfulmastermind.com**

I LOVE hearing about what people are creating around their life interests!  It is exhilarating to see people taking action to move forward in the direction that brings them joy and passion in life!

*Please share your passion with me at:*

*Juanita@AudaciousMarketingMastery.com*

*CHAPTER NOTES*

## CHAPTER FOUR

# CHANGING YOUR CHILD'S DISRESPECT INTO RESPECT

# Kathy Holperin

Kath was a stay-at-home mom for 15 years before starting her coaching business: **Life Coach Kathy Holperin, LLC**. She greatly enjoys group coaching others to discern their own and one another's gifts, parent coaching and individual coaching. Life experience and the coaching skills gained through being a student of The Coaching Institute provide a solid foundation for Kath to coach moms to be all they can be. Her passion is teaching them skills and providing guidance to discover the ways of life that reflect who they are in a more joyful, balanced and passionate way.

Kath and her husband of 18 years share in the joys of raising an almost teenage daughter and two teenage sons. Aside from the joys of raising her family and having a breakfast date with her husband once a week, she is an avid reader, considers walking with her girlfriends sacred, loves to cross-country ski and dabbles in many other activities such as photography, knitting, playing Scrabble® and snowmobiling. She and her family make their home in beautiful Northern Wisconsin where the seasons are as diverse as our own children.

If you would like to learn how to effectively balance your life call or email Coach Kath to set up a free 30 minute conditional consultation.

## Kathy Holperin

**Eagle River, WI • (877) 477-2801 • coachkath@verizon.net**

Change is the best
At our own behest.

It will pass the test.
If we model the rest.

Kathy Holperin

## CHANGING YOUR CHILD'S DISRESPECT INTO RESPECT

T his chapter presents guiding principles on how to teach our children to be more respectful. I chose this topic after interviewing parents and asking them, "What is one thing that you would like to change about your children?" The majority said that they would like their kids to be more respectful to them and others. A frequent comment heard was, "If I'd have talked to my parents the way my kids talk to me, I'd have been slapped!" Times have definitely changed.

Many parents are at a loss as to how to handle various situations. Perhaps you endured physical consequences for your actions and were demanded to act and behave in certain ways, so you did, out of fear. Time has taught us that those consequences are not healthy for our children's self-esteem so the pendulum of parenting techniques has swung in the opposite direction in some homes. Thus, in insuring our children have a healthier self-esteem we may let them get away with certain behaviors, coddle them and cater to their every want and desire. We expect them to be thankful for all we do for them but it's never enough and the disrespect continues. We get frustrated and overwhelmed, not knowing what to do. We become exasperated and resort to using the methods our parents may have used, then feel guilty afterwards because we know that really doesn't work either.

How *are* our children disrespecting us? They may ignore us when we ask them to clean their bedrooms, unload the dishwasher or take out the trash. They leave garbage and dirty dishes lying around in the living room when we specifically asked them not to eat in there. They interrupt us while we are on the telephone. They neglect to call us and let us know they arrived at their destination safely. *And* they roll their eyes at us when we want to share our words of wisdom with them. At our wits end, we scream, "Things are going to start changing around here and THIS TIME I MEAN IT!!!!"

Do you really mean it? Do you know what to do to make those changes happen? Are you just going to yell louder the next time you want things to get done? Are you going to take away all their privileges so they know that you mean business? Or are you going to fall into the same old routine and ask yourself over and over again, "Why doesn't anybody *listen* to me???" And that, my friend, is the exact behavior we want to change! How do we get our kids to listen to us? We must first *listen to them*!

Let's start by defining **Respect:** noun. 2.) an act of giving particular attention; consideration 3.) high or special regard: esteem. **Respect**: verb. a.) to consider worthy of high regard; esteem b.) to refrain from interfering with.

Wow, wouldn't we all like more of this in our lives!! How many of you are craving *particular attention to* or *consideration of your thoughts and feelings*! We are so busy in our lives with homes, spouses, children, their activities, our activities and our own self-care that we sometimes forget about core values like holding each other in high esteem. Is not our ultimate job on this planet to build others up and let them know how valuable they are in our lives and in the lives of others? Do we feel valuable ourselves? Yes, *you* are valuable. More than you may realize at this moment—know and appreciate that about yourself! No one else has the exact same personality traits, physical traits, thoughts, feelings and experiences to draw from. That's what makes you, you! And the same goes for our children. Perhaps long ago you didn't feel valued when you got slapped across the face or told to go change the outfit that you were so proud of picking out yourself. Or you drew a picture that you thought was absolutely beautiful and all someone else could see in it was a minor detail that was left out.

We all want and need to feel valued. OK, now reread the definition of respect and imagine what that would look like in your household. Also, keep in mind what *is* already working in your home. We have a tendency to think about what is not working and overlook all the wonderful, positive actions we are already taking. How would you like your children to be responding to you and others? Is this being modeled for them in your other relationships? What needs to be done differently to make that happen?

It is important to know that we cannot change the core of our children. And neither can others change *our* core: who we are at our centers and inner most being, the part of us with genuine likes and dislikes, and desires. However, we can work towards bringing out their best. How do we bring forth their best? By modeling and bringing out our best! We all have the necessary tools to change our circumstances, and the first tool we need is a strong desire to really "change things around here." You may have a desire for or strong intuition for things to be better, which is why you purchased this book – because you are ready for some change! I truly believe there can be peace on earth and it must start from within. We *can not* demand it, we must model it. This quote says it all,

**"We must be the change we want to see in the world."** – Gandhi

The thought you are having about this "not being easy" is accurate but trust that with a healthy commitment and a little time, we can take small steps to build a home full of respect for one another. Sometimes you will forget to use your new tools, so forgive yourself and try again the next time. After all, there is no such thing as failure, just feedback when it comes to apparent mistakes. If something doesn't go as you had hoped, ask yourself-What have I learned from this experience and what can I do differently when in a similar situation?

What are these new tools needed to earn more respect from our children? The first one is **"focused listening."** What is focused listening? It is the ability to put your own agenda, thoughts and feelings aside and truly tune into what your child is saying or not saying. Listen for the feeling behind their words, and look at what their body language may be telling you. Reflect back to your child what you are hearing to make sure you understand them correctly. Here's an example...

You are trying to make dinner, and just realized that there aren't any spaghetti noodles in the cupboard. You have to leave in 45 minutes to take your eleven- year-old son to soccer practice, the water is boiling and the spaghetti sauce is sputtering and splattering all over the stove. You've had a hectic day at work. Your nine-year-old daughter comes running into the kitchen. "Mom, Mom, look at this new magic trick I learned!" You *react*: "Not now, I'm in the middle of making dinner. I don't have time right now!" Your daughter stomps her feet. "You never have time, you're always too busy!" and runs out of the room into her bedroom, slamming the door behind her. You might yell back, "How many times have I told you not to slam the door!"  The same scenario seems to take place night after night.

Things *can* improve from this all too common scenario. According to the late Dr. Robert S. Hartman,  people will hold back as much as 40% of their capacity to be productive and cooperative until they feel valued as human beings.  Wow, that's a lot!!  I'd like my family to be more cooperative!  So what other steps can we take to bring on cooperation and productivity?

It is best to take care of matters *as* we encounter them.  If we continue in old patterns of reacting based on stress levels, we could be doing a lot of repair work down the road when it comes to our personal relationships.  The best-way to handle the above situation would be to actually pause and truly listen to what your daughter had to say.  You may want to turn off the spaghetti sauce first, but stop what you are doing, look her in the eye and give her your full attention.  This takes both patience and practice!  You could respond by saying, "So, you learned a new magic trick today, I can tell you are quite excited about this!"  (Just imagine how your child will feel!) It's a win-win situation. You honestly may not have the time to watch her magic trick, but you acknowledged her and who she is at her core, a little girl excited about learning magic tricks.  Next you might explain in a **calm neutral tone** that you would like to see her magic trick; however, now is not a good time. Would she be able to wait until after you bring her brother home from soccer practice, or would she like to ride with and show you once you arrive at your destination?  Notice how she was given a choice here so she could feel some healthy control over the situation.  It's important you follow through and let her know when you are able to watch her perform.  Then she will begin to trust your word when you follow through on what you say you are going to do.  By **co-creating the solution** of watching her magic later when she chooses a time that is more convenient for the two of you, she is also learning patience and probably feeling more grown up because you talked civilly to her, which in turn will yield more cooperation from her. And RESPECT.

Of course the child best learns these skills if both parents are practicing them, which leads me to another aspect of teaching respect to your children.  **Are you setting the example**?  How are you and your spouse/significant other treating each other?   Children learn best by our example. If we are demanding one thing of them and doing another, they will have very little respect for us or our wishes. Here's a recent example from my own household:   I asked my fourteen-year-old son to clean his bedroom because I couldn't tolerate looking at the mess anymore. He called me in there and said, "Why should I clean my room? Do you know what yours looks like right now?" We went into my room. I was relieved that I had at least made the bed that morning. He pointed out the basket of odds and ends that had been sitting behind the door for the past couple of months, the heap of clothes piled on a storage bin in my closet that could be worn again or thrown down the laundry chute, the worn clothes my husband had stacked on his chair, and my stack of books lying on the floor next to the nightstand.

Some of you may be shocked that I allowed my son to talk to me that way and let him take me into my own room to point out my own little messes. But I knew in my heart that he was just taking after us (the apple doesn't fall far from the tree) and I can't get mad at him for some behavior we, his parents, modeled. Doesn't that just make you cringe, when your kids humble you like that!? However, I took the opportunity to explain to him that although our bedroom wasn't perfect, neither did I expect his to be but there were some limits to what we considered acceptable such as; his dad and I put our garbage *in* the garbage can, not on the floor, and at least put the clothes down the chute or off the floor were the dog isn't going to make a bed out of them and it feels nice to climb into a made bed in the evening. Of course you, the reader, are free to set your own standards of living these are just some of ours I shared with our son.

Furthermore, we have to respect that our children are unique with likes and dislikes very different from our own. (We chose to not make a big deal out of whether or not he makes his bed.) It is unreasonable to expect them to eat all the same foods that we like or wear the same style of clothing. Celebrate their uniqueness! I once bought a beautiful navy blue backpack with little flowers all over it for my daughter when she was quite young. I thought it was so cute and that she'd absolutely love it! Boy was I wrong! She thought it was ugly and she wasn't going to use it. And that was that, she informed me as she threw it on the ground. At the time I probably tried to convince her that it was cute and that she was going to use it whether she liked it or not. I never once considered that she might prefer one with the cartoon character Arthur or his little sister D.W. on it. I shared this story with a wise woman at the time and she said to me, "She has a right to her emotions and desires; it's her behavior she has to learn to control." Wow, did I need to hear that! I thought people always had to be thankful for what they had and if they didn't like it, too bad! At least she had a backpack. It was yet another great learning opportunity for the two of us, as I showed her some **mutual respect** at a time when we were both calm and I said, "Honey, I realize that you don't like the backpack. I should have let you help pick one out but this is the one we have right now so I'd like you to use it this school year. Then next year we can pick one out that you like." How do you think a child would feel after being talked to like that versus being controlled and told how she should feel?

It is also important to **focus on what is right and working.** The other day my 16-year-old son had an incident with the neighbor up the hill. My son had recently built a wooden box in which to mount a sub-woofer. He keeps it in the trunk of his car (my husband and I set a limit here and wouldn't allow this until he had his license for at least six months and was incident free as we feel the loud music could be a large distraction to a recently licensed driver). It's a really *bumpin'* ride now, in his terms. He's helped a friend install his sound system, and then they built a box for another friend with a few other boys taking notes on the procedure. I was in awe with their skill level and confidence using the tools to build the big, wooden crate. The bass was going on and off most of the afternoon but I really didn't think anything of it as I was focused on what was working; their productivity and skill. Now, I regard myself as a considerate person. I know when I have to set other limits, especially with noise in the neighborhood, however, a neighbor had had enough. He drove to our house and very civilly asked the boys to "turn down the bass" as he'd been listening to it all day. Later, I commented to my son that it was unfortunate that he couldn't appreciate what he was doing yet I could relate about annoying sounds as I listened to a dog barking in the distance for quite sometime early that morning. My son's comment focused on what was right and working by saying, "At least he knew it was 'bass'! He could have told us to stop making all that 'noise'!" My son chose to decide it was all right because he used the correct term regarding the output of the speaker and, more than likely, because he asked him respectfully to tone it down.

Speaking of making choices, I am reminded of an experience with my daughter last winter. She wanted to walk with a friend about a mile to the nearest video store to rent a movie. Although it was spring there was still a lot of snow on the ground, especially in the cemetery that we walk through as it's a significant shortcut. I noticed when she was getting ready to leave that she had on tennis shoes. I considered telling her to put her boots on but then I decided to let her experience the natural consequence of walking with tennis shoes in deep snow. I was tired of nagging and controlling to get my kids to do what I thought they should do. I told her she was to be home within 45 minutes and to take a cell phone with her. She wasn't home yet when the time was up but she called me to tell me where she was at and that she'd be home in about three minutes. I thanked her for calling me and paying attention to the time. And then she said, "Boy was I stupid, Mom! I wore my tennis shoes and we cut through the cemetery and I got snow in my shoes and now my feet are freezing! The next time I walk to the video store, I'm wearing my boots!" What a great lesson! She learned to wear her boots outside while there's still snow on the ground, and I remembered to trust that my kids are smart enough to learn some things on their own without me opening my mouth!

I have observed that children often show disrespect because they are overwhelmed and may lack the tools to respond in a healthy fashion. We need to remember to pay attention to what they may be feeling that would be bringing on the misbehavior. Is it possible they don't feel heard and understood? When they don't feel heard and understood it is difficult to expect them to do the same to others. Are they unable to express their needs? Is something else bothering them and they have no clue how to resolve the issue or do they even know that resolution is a choice? Are they burnt out trying to live up to someone else's standards?

**In order to model respect for our children, consider asking yourself these questions:**

- Is there a healthy balance in my life between self-care, family and friends, and work?
- Am I able to express my feelings in such a way that I am being considerate to others even when I am angry, tired or misunderstood?
- Do I feel heard and understood by others?
- How would it feel to be understood and accepted by others simply for who I am at this moment?
- Am I able to express my needs and see that they are met?
- Do I know how to handle a conflict and bring it on to resolution?
- Am I living the life I want or living up to other people's standards for my *life*?
- Am I setting healthy boundaries and limits based on my personal values?

**Now turn the tables:**

- Is there a healthy balance in my child's life…

- Are they able to express their feelings…

Keep going – you get the picture…

A lot of us parents weren't raised with the skills needed to answer the above questions positively. So if we don't learn the skills and model them for our children, how can we expect our kids to express themselves in a healthy manner, with respect for themselves and others?

I hope I have provided some valuable insight for you. This most of all: In order to gain respect from our children, we have to model it. And trust that they have the tools within them to grow up to model respect for the next generation.

*Peace to you and your household! Life Coach Kathy Holperin, LLC*

# CHAPTER NOTES

# In Her Power

SECTION TWO

# PEACE

---

## CHAPTER FIVE

# WHY HEAL?
# ONE WOMAN'S TESTIMONY OF
# HEALING, FAITH, AND FREEDOM

# LaTalya Palmer-Lewis

LaTalya Palmer-Lewis, is an Empowerment Specialist, Coach and Trainer. She is excitingly the founder of "Get Your Life Back on Track-Life Purpose Coaching for Women"

LaTalya has an abundance of experience working with women in healing and growth and is also a wife, mother of four children and an entrepreneur. Her focus is helping women move beyond the challenges and obstacles that stand in the way of fulfilling their soul's purpose and heart desires; and "Get Back on Track" in the midst of balancing professional, school, and/or family.

*LaTalya* is also a Professional Development Training Consultant and Founder of **Personal Growth for Professionals Inc.,** an agency that conducts personal and professional growth & development trainings and workshops for Human Service Agencies.

As a coach, LaTalya brings her intimate experience of balancing, reclaiming herself and "Getting Back on Track". Along with her professional training and personal experiences, LaTalya's studies in Spiritual and Life Coaching, helps her bring a holistic approach; a combination of spiritual, emotional, mental and physical support tools to enhance life long transformation to her clients. Her approach focuses on the individual as a whole being. She believes that with the appropriate support and tools for empowerment, each being has the inner capability to move beyond limiting beliefs and begin living the life he or she deserves!

Life's obstacles don't have to become a blockage; let them be a tool to create the new you! Get Your Life Back on Track TODAY!

## LaTalya Palmer-Lewis

**Greenbelt, MD • 301-345-0095• safespacecoaching@yahoo.ca**

Get your life back

And on track.


Make your power within,

Be the power,

Without which you are nothing.

LaTalya Palmer-Lewis

## WHY HEAL?

## ONE WOMAN'S TESTIMONY OF HEALING, FAITH AND FREEDOM

Throughout history women have been revered and cursed, exalted and burned, acclaimed and condemned for their innate and powerful ability to heal oneself, their family, their community and the world. Our psyches have been conflicted from the start. However, the unwavering truth is that, from goddesses to priestesses; bush women to witches, from mothers to midwives, the female energy are a powerful presence that has an abundance of Good to contribute to the planet. However, as a result of the constant degradation of our womanhood many of us have lost touch with our innate power. Instead of nurturing, developing and sharing our great inheritances we suppress and even sometimes despise them.

During countless conversations with friends, women in my support groups and clients, I empathically listen to women who are in tangled webs of their hurtful past searching for a way out. Conversely, with this desperate plea for support also comes the inevitable hesitancy and resistance. Questions such as, "Why heal? Why bring up all that stuff from my past only to live it all over again? It's dead buried and gone. Why bring up all the pain I've fought so hard to forget? Is it worth the trouble?" naturally begin to surface. Undoubtedly, these women are not alone. Consequently, I will share with you excerpts of personal experiences resulting in a powerful testimony of how the path of healing has changed my life. It is my prayer and intention that within these next few pages, you will find your own answers to some of these questions, along with the inspiration and support you need to move to the next level of your journey.

## LOSING INNOCENCE

Can you remember things that were said to you or around you about being a girl, things about your body, sexuality or looks while you were growing up? Were they mostly positive or negative? Did some remarks or statements stand out for you more than others? What were some statements you heard? The most memorable comment for me came when I was around 7 or 8, while sitting at the dinner table with my mother, father and younger brother. Just to give you a little background, I had a beautiful navy blue, a-line dress with red skates as a print and a red bow tie that my aunt made for me. I loved this dress but it was a size too big around the stomach area. Well one night while eating dinner, I told them that one of my classmates told me I looked pregnant with the dress on. I thought it was rather funny, even silly. But they were very offended and somehow seemed insulted. My father belted out, "you are disgusting", my mother yelled, "You are so nasty". Their faces were of disgust and disbelief. I was horrified. I couldn't believe they took it in such a bad way. I somehow associated their disgust to my body and sexuality, thus, another layer of shame.

Can you recall what your parents or guardians like in regard to women? How were the women around you treated? How did they refer to them or address them? Were they respected or scorned? How about you? How were you treated as a young girl? Were you taught to honor yourself? Do you remember any specific incidents that had detrimental affects on the way you saw yourself? How does it affect you now? As a child I witnessed my mother run from one abusive relationship to the next. I watched her suffer at the hands of the men she knew and loved. They treated her poorly and she remained loyal to the pain and abuse. I could never figure out why such a smart, beautiful and strong woman tolerated such maltreatment.

From the tender age of six my own childhood was fraught with senseless and cruel acts of violation and abuse. The consequential hurt, pain and confusion I felt was too much for me to bear. My mind, heart and body needed relief so I tried my hand at every remedy my young mind knew. Unfortunately, to my dismay, I learned that simple childhood cures like band-aides and chicken-noodle soup could not cure feelings of horror, shock, hurt and unspeakable pain. Nor could a daily dose of Tylenol rid my mind of the on-going migraines or help me to make sense of the techno-color memories that haunted my mind. Because I was forced into silence, I had no one to turn to or provide me the relief and comfort I needed. As a result, I spent innumerable days and countless nights wallowing in loneliness, shame and guilt. The shadows of abuse and feelings of lewdness traveled with me everywhere I went. I internalized these erroneous feelings and thoughts of myself until they became an intricate part of my being.

According to T. Harv Ecker, our subconscious is conditioned through verbal programming, modeling and specific incidents. At an early age we are programmed to relate to ourselves and the world in a particular manner. From the things I heard, saw and experienced, my foundation was set for self-hate and low-expectations. Thus, this is the way I treated myself and allowed others to treat me until I circumvented the pattern.

## THE AWAKENING

As you may already know, it's not unusual that the suffering of a significant person or your own repeated patterns of dysfunction can help you become aware that something in your life needs to change. Awareness is a pivotal point in your process. You are making your first step out of victim hood and are now in the position of power. At your command is the power to make life changing choices and decisions that will help you shift your current situation. The birth of my daughter was that critical point for me. For a long time I knew I needed help, I knew that if I kept harboring this untold pain I would surely continue the cycle of self-destruction. The dysfunctional relationships were evidence that I was unconsciously reliving the pains of my past. I full of rage and apathy. The person I'd become was not the person I knew I could be. Deep inside I was really a loving person who wanted to be good and live a fulfilled life. I just thought the way I was living was normal.

The birth of my daughter gave me a new found passion for life and reason to live, not just merely survive but to truly LIVE. When I saw her something in me came alive. I began to remember that life is meant to be enjoyed. A spark of light and innocence within me was touched. I knew I had to make a change. It was time for me to release the fear of the unknown, time to step out and make my life an act of faith. Faith in the silent truth, that I had the light and power within me to shine and live a courageous life. A life filled

71

with loving relationships, a purposeful career, personal fulfillment, and creative endeavors that support my community and the world. If I was to break the cycles of the past and create a healthy life for myself and my child, it was imperative that I find a way out.

## RECLAIMING MY LIFE

Through researching, law of attraction and God's grace I found different levels, avenues and methods of healing that changed my life. Through trial, error and constant imbalance, ironically I learned that in order to find balance I had to focus on healing my spiritual, mental, emotional and physical aspects of self.

According to Shakti Gawain, The Four Levels of Healing, "The spiritual level provides a foundation for the development of all other levels." We facilitate our spiritual healing through any activity or practice that cultivates our soul. Prayer, meditation, truth teachings, song and dance are among the activities that have supported me in this process. In our healing lies the opportunity to unearth the dormant but ever present Power of Life within us. It opens us to our true Self that will guide and provides us with the love, support, peace and comfort we need throughout our path. This Power works within us to realign us with our Source of health, wealth, abundance and well-being.

Our emotional and mental healing is necessary so that we can feel whole and fulfilled within ourselves. We learn to accept and be present with our host of human feelings, have greater access to our intuition, which enables us to connect with one another in safer and more fulfilling ways. As we develop our emotional and mental bodies, we increase our capacity to enjoy life, relationships, our sexual nature, careers, and other growth oriented opportunities.

Esther and Jerry Hicks authors of "Ask and It Is Given" suggest that our feelings are the point of attraction for experiences in our life and our emotions are indicators of what we are about to experience. Thus, when we learn to raise our vibration, we awaken our power to transform our experiences. This is also why our mental healing is so important. Our prominent thought determines what we feel lead to our actions. This ultimately results in our behavior or outcomes.

I often wondered why bad things happened to good people. Even though I did good things for other people, many areas of my life were still unfruitful. I had people in my circle that lied to and betrayed me. I participated in relationships with people who took advantage of my giving nature. The injustices go on and on. But further education made me cognizant of how natural law governs our universe and ultimately my personal life. I learned to integrate principles such as; as above, so below; as within, so it is without, what goes up must come down, opposites, polarities; and it led me to

73

see that these laws are impersonal. Just as, if a human being and a rock are thrown off of a roof both will fall to the ground. In accordance with the law of gravity it can be no other way. Like a bright light shone on me after years of darkness; with this enlightment came the realization that I was responsible for my feelings, relationships and situations in my life.

Therefore, whether I am focusing on my fears or my possibilities; whether I expect the best or the worst in a situation, like a human magnet, I always draw to me whichever feeling was dominant. Consequently, since I concluded long ago that I was a victim; I continuously but unconsciously created situations and people in my experiences to confirm these etched in beliefs. The key for me was to learn to gradually shift my thoughts, beliefs, attitudes, and focus so that I was able to draw more desirable experiences in my life.

And lastly but of equal importance is our physical aspect. Our body is the temple that keeps us planted on this physical earth. Our fulfillment, mobility and to the extent that we can enjoy life's riches has a great deal to do with our physical state. Our mental state, emotional state, foods we eat and our natural environment all have a great deal to do with our physical state. As a young adult I suffered from anemia, migraines, severe menstrual cramps, hemorrhaging, among other things. Stress was an ongoing state of being for me. For a 20 year old, I felt very old in my body. One year

I received a book that saved my life. My aunt sent me a book entitled, "Heal Thyself" by Queen Afua. Queen Afua is a holistic healer among many other wonderful things. Through her book, I was introduced to a natural way of living. I learned about natural juices, vegetarian foods, fruits and vegetables that are used to heal different symptoms and diseases. I was in awe. From that time I went on a path of healing and purification of my mind, body and soul through foods and juices. I can testify that the results were amazing. My whole outlook on my body and health changed. As I ingested life given herbs and cleansers, I released toxic emotions that made a home within. My transformation was astonishing. I began to feel youthful energetic, my health began to progress, I'd never felt so good. Another awesome result was that every other aspect of my life improved as well. My spiritual connection became stronger, my emotions were balanced and my mind was sharper, clearer and focused.

## THE JOURNEY CONTINUES...

Though it has taken me years of spiritual healing, professional support, love from myself, family and friends; I am proud of where I am and my journey is still unfolding and flourishing. It is an exciting and worthwhile way of life that frees me from the programming and conditioning of the past and allows me to live in the present moment. I am able to enjoy time with myself; my children; have a healthy relationship with my husband; do fantastic work that I love, and create time for important things and people in my life.

If you feel so inspired there are many you can do to begin your own journey. Silent moments, mindfulness, prayer, meditation, physical exercise, healthier diet, rest, consciously breathing are some activities that you can perform to begin moving in the direction you want to go. Although in-person professional and spiritual support is recommended, there are many books on the market that can support you on your journey. With healing happiness, joy, abundance, great relationships, a light heart, and so much more are all possible. We all have greatness that has a right to shine. We all have a life that is truly divine. Our purpose and gifts may differ but we are all equally important in this lifetime. So go forward - Claim your wholeness, your healing, your freedom and your power.

*Stay Blessed! LaTalya Palmer-Lewis*

# CHAPTER NOTES

## CHAPTER SIX

## A Legacy For Your Daughter: Improving Your Body Image For Your Daughter's Sake

# MARTYN A. DELL

Martyn A. Dell is the founder of Joyful Changes Coaching, a coaching practice that specializes in coaching teen girls between the ages of 13 and 19. Life experiences coupled with coaching skills from the Coaching Institute have created a passion for helping teen girls expand the beauty, strength, and confidence already inherent in themselves.

Prior to becoming a coach, Martyn gained 15 years of customer service experience in various fields such as library, retail, call centre, law, and non-profit organizations. Coaching is Martyn's way of making a contribution to the world.

As a member of the Night Owls, Martyn has co-authored an e-book entitled "Marketing for the Totally Terrified" which takes the fear out of marketing a business. Through learning a new way of marketing her coaching services, Martyn moved from being Totally Terrified into Marvelously Motivated.

Martyn lives in London, Ontario with her beautiful tortoiseshell kitty, Cocoa. She loves reading young adult books, music, sewing, and yoga.

## Martyn A. Dell

**London, Ontario • 519-672-8013• www.JoyfulChangesCoaching.com**

Your body? Love it.

Your life? Love it.

Any griefs, any sorrows? Reframe it.

Your life? Love it.

Lovingly.

Martyn A. Dell

# A LEGACY FOR YOUR DAUGHTER: IMPROVING YOUR BODY IMAGE FOR YOUR DAUGHTER'S SAKE

Do you often look in the mirror and hate what you see? Do you think your butt's too big, flat, saggy, or round? Do you hate your thighs? Are your boobs heading south and your wrinkles heading north? Are you constantly making disparaging remarks about your appearance? Guess who's watching you? Your daughter! Your son is too but this chapter will deal with the mother-daughter connection (since I have a mother and am a daughter.) Because mothers and daughters have the same body parts, there is a special bond between them that is joyful, complex, and often painful. I'd like to share with you how this relationship can be a little more peaceful for both of you.

We all want what's best for our children. One of the goals we have for our kids is to have them to grow up to be independent, productive, happy members of society. Sometimes we fail at this goal when we have daughters that grow up to dislike the way that they look. When someone dislikes their appearance it affects every aspect of their lives. I would have to say that it poisons their very existence.

Where do you suppose this negative self image came from? It came from us. Research shows that girls get most of their self image from their mothers. If their mothers dislike the way that they look in the mirror chances are that their daughters will dislike their own looks as well. Research has also shown that mothers with high self esteem often have daughters with high self esteem too.

Currently, the media plays a huge part in women's self esteem issues. It pervades every aspect of our lives. It's on our TVs, in our music, in our magazines, and it's on billboards. The messages are everywhere! Basically they tells us that we are not good enough, smart enough, pretty enough, or handsome enough. These messages hammer us every day and destroy our self image. They tell us that we must be perfect. Guess what? Perfection doesn't exist. It is an illusion. It preys on those of us that are vulnerable to the message that if we are not perfect, we are not worthy of love, respect, kindness, or even life.

It is into this atmosphere of body negativity that we bring a beautiful baby daughter. That daughter that looks up to you as a role model will most likely grow up having the same beliefs and attitudes about her body that you do about yours. Do you want your daughter to hate her body if you hate yours? Of course not! I'd like to share some ideas with you that might help you see your body in a whole different light so you can share that love with your daughter.

But first, let me share a bit of my story with you so you can see where I'm coming from.

## WHO IS MARTYN?

I grew up in rural Ontario in the 70's and 80's. My father was very loving and I was very close to him. My mother, on the other hand, was very negative and controlling. There was and still is a great deal of conflict between her and I.

I was a normal baby and toddler. My baby pictures show a cute little girl with big blue eyes. Just after I turned 6, I had my tonsils and adenoids removed. I hemorrhaged on the operating table and almost died from the loss of blood. Apparently I lost a gallon of blood from my tiny body.

After I recovered, I started gaining weight. I look back at the few pictures of my childhood and I was chubby but by no means was I obese. To my mother, though, I was a disgusting slob. There are many hurtful, cruel things that she has said to me over the years that I will probably never forget. Looking back now, I can see that she loved me in her own way but she didn't know how to show it. She meant the best for me but didn't know how to deal with a fat daughter. Her method of trying to get me to lose weight was to humiliate and ridicule me. It didn't work. Criticism is never a good motivator! It destroys your self image and breaks your spirit.

Mom took me to the doctor when I was 10 and I was put on diet pills. I was a 10-year old on speed. I didn't understand at the time why I had headaches and was jumpy and twitchy. Speed will do that to you!

This started the cycle of yo yo dieting that remained with me for the next 10 years. I would lose the weight and then gain it all back plus more. Each time I regained the weight I felt like the biggest failure. My mother controlled every morsel of food that went into my mouth. I became a closet eater as a way to rebel against her. I would eat candy compulsively in my room at night. I would use all of my allowance to buy candy at school and I would eat all of it. It never seemed to be enough to fill the void in me that should have been filled with my mother's unconditional love.

Now that I can look back in hindsight, she had a very negative self image that she tried to pass on to me. It worked! I can remember looking in the mirror when I was a teenager and wishing I was dead. I hated myself so much that I wanted to end my life. I was so miserable and ashamed of myself that I couldn't see the way out. I'm not sure how much of this was normal teenage angst but I doubt that wanting to do away with yourself was normal.

Thankfully, I was befriended by a neighbour who listened to me, accepted me as I was, and loved me for who I was on the inside and not what I looked like on the outside. Susan lived down the road from me and wanted me to help her with her housework on Friday nights. There were many nights that she just listened to me talk about my worries, hopes, and dreams. She was there for me when my father died when I was 19. I will never forget the unconditional love she showed me. She was a wonderful, positive female role model for me at a time that I desperately needed one.

When I began college I finally started to come into my own. I was away from my mother's influence and I began to decide for myself how I wanted to live my life. I had a large circle of friends and an active social life for the first time ever. I was finally with people that overlooked my size and saw the person I was beneath. I loved my college years!

In my early 20s, as I was about to begin another diet, a wise doctor told me bluntly to make a decision whether I wanted to fail with another diet or learn to accept myself. I was horrified at the prospect. What, me give up dieting? But I'd been dieting since I was 10 years old. It was pretty much all I knew. I was pretty ticked off at that doctor but she changed my life that day!

When I thought about it, I realized that I was not really living. I had so much body hatred that I was just going through the motions of enjoying my life. I wasn't really living it. I decided to get off the diet roller coaster and start accepting myself as I was instead of how I would be when I lost the weight. Dieting never worked for me since I would lose the weight and gain even more back.

A year of therapy helped me put some perspective into my childhood and helped me to tame some of the demons that I carried around with me from the emotional abuse. I believe that therapy helped me mature and gave me a starting point for the person I was meant to be.

What also helped me grow as a person was getting fired from my first post-college job after 5 1/2 years. I got fired for having a bad attitude. I hated myself and everybody else. It was the best thing that could have happened to me. At that point I had the freedom to decide what I wanted to do with my life so I went back to college for another diploma.

At college the second time my confidence soared as I was earning top grades. This college career was devoted to academics as my first one was devoted to the social aspects. Both were absolutely crucial for my development.

I've done a great deal of self analysis in the past 20 years to find out what make me special and unique. It has been a struggle at times but the journey has also been joyful. I have learned to like what I see in the mirror most of the time (I have to be honest and tell you that there are still days I look in the mirror and go Yuck! Thankfully, those days are few and far between.) I strongly believe that this journey to self acceptance is neverending. I will always be learning about myself and learning to accept myself. I still have scars from my childhood but at least they aren't open wounds anymore.

My relationship with my mother is civil. It's a superficial one, and while that makes me sad not to have a close bond with the woman that gave birth to me, it is for self protection that I keep her at arms length. The less she knows about my life the less she can criticize me for the choices I make. She still nags me about my weight every chance she gets but now the barbs don't wound me as much as they did when I was younger. I have the ability to be assertive with her and tell her when she is out of line. When she crosses the line, the conversation is over.

## SO WITHOUT FURTHER ADO, HERE ARE 10 THINGS YOU SHOULD NEVER SAY TO YOUR DAUGHTER:

1. You are too fat to get a boyfriend because boys don't like fat girls (not true, by the way, I've had several boyfriends!)
2. No one is going to hire you unless they can stick you in the back room (also not true, since I've had several positions dealing with the public directly.)
3. You're too fat to go out for Halloween (no child wants to hear this, especially when they are only 10 years old. I still hate Halloween!)

4. You don't need that! (referring to any food that is not considered "diet" food. Well, I want it so I'm going to have it.)

5. If you lose X amount of weight, I'll buy you a new wardrobe (bribery gets you nowhere.)

6. Look at that fat tummy! (at the same time as touching said tummy. Hello! Can we say boundary issues!)

7. You would be so pretty if only you lost weight (why do I have to lose weight to be pretty? Am I a dog now?)

8. You look like a potato sack tied in the middle in that dress (Hey! I loved that dress. If you don't like it, don't look!)

9. Will yoga help you lose weight? (Um, mom, that's not the point of yoga.)

10. I always loved your brother more than I loved you because he just snuggled into me when he was a baby and YOU just cried (Ouch! That one hurt! This is wrong in so many ways.)

**NOW THAT WE'VE GOT THE NASTY STUFF OUT OF THE WAY, LET'S LOOK AT SOME THINGS THAT YOUR DAUGHTER WOULD LOVE TO HEAR FROM YOU:**

1. You are beautiful just as you are and the right boy will see that. (If he doesn't see it then he is not worthy of you!)

2. I love you! (this cannot be said too often. My mother never told me she loved me until after my father died.)

3. You can do, be, and have anything that you want. There is a whole world out there just waiting for you.

4. Every body is different and that's what makes us all beautiful. Beauty comes in all shapes and sizes (life would be boring if we all looked the same.)

5. The beauty within is more important than outside beauty (would you rather have an awesome personality and average looks or a nasty personality and be gorgeous?)

6. Everyone feels self conscious about some part of their body (this is perfectly normal)

7. The pictures of models that you see in magazines are airbrushed. They don't really look like that. It's all fake!

8. Dieting is NOT healthy. It is better to eat healthier and exercise moderately and your weight will be perfect for you. (Diets do NOT work!)

9. The average American female is 5'4" and weighs 144 lbs.

10. Your body is a miracle! Love it!


So you might be asking yourself, what can I do to improve my self esteem so I can be a good role model for my daughter? Here is a handy checklist of things that have helped me. They just might help you.

## 1. PRACTICE AN ATTITUDE OF GRATITUDE

What I found really helpful was to make a list each day of things I'm grateful for. I also count the blessings in my life and the things I love about myself. What this practice does is to take the focus off of the negative things in my life and makes me aware of all the good things I have going on around and in me. This is the Law of Attraction at work. The Law of Attraction states that what we give our energy, attention, and focus to is what we get whether it is positive or negative. Of course, I want the positive!

For more information on the Law of Attraction check out the works of Michael Losier (http://www.lawofattractionbook.com/) and Eva Gregory (http://www.feelgoodguidetoprosperity.com)

## 2. THROW OUT THOSE BATHROOM SCALES

Do you really need something telling you what you weigh? But you may be saying I need to know the actual number. The truth is you don't actually need to know it - you want to know it. There is a difference. Does it really matter in the grand scheme of things if you've gained or lost five pounds? Will the world be better if you just lost that last five pounds? Probably not. You would just take up a tiny bit less space.

What these pieces of plastic and metal do is make us feel falsely proud or ashamed of ourselves depending on the numbers.

The numbers on a scale do not determine if we are a good person or not. They can't tell us that we are kind to other people or that we are well loved by our friends and family. They are just hunks of plastic and metal. I say, GET RID OF THE SCALES!

If you decided that this is something that you absolutely cannot do, at least do not make comments about your numbers, either positive or negative, around your daughter. Try to limit weighing yourself to once a day, once a week, once a month, or only at the doctor's office. Measure your weight by how your clothes feel on you rather than by numbers on the scale. Believe me, you'll feel better for it.

## 3. DO NOT DIET!

Let's face it, most of us have been on at least one diet in our lives. Tell me, did it work? Probably not. It's been well documented that 95% of all diets fail. That means that only 5% of people dieting continue to keep the weight off. Most only keep it off for 5 years. The diet industry wants us to fail because then we keep buying more pills, products, books, and gadgets. That's why the American diet industy is a billion dollar industry. They feed off of our starvation!

Keeping the weight off often comes at a great sacrifice. You can't eat the foods that you want and when you are deprived it's all you can think about. This is food obsession at it's worst. I don't know about you but when I get hungry, I feel nauseous and if it goes on too long I get a splitting headache. This is hardly conducive to being a productive member of society.

Dieting, taken to the extreme, can lead to eating disorders like anorexia and bulimia. It can also lead to compulsive overeating like I had as a teenager. We all know that teenagers are vulnerable to eating disorders. A lot of this can be laid at the feet of the media, peer pressure, and sadly enough, parental expectations. The desire/obsession to be thin is really ruining a lot of lives unnecessarily.

It is absolutely crucial that you display a healthy attitude towards food. There are no good or bad foods. There are foods that are less nutritious than others, certainly, but all foods can be part of a healthy eating plan. As the nutritionists say, "moderation is key." This means have a piece of cake but don't eat the whole cake! Eat more fruits and veggies and less pop, candy, and chips. By showing your daughter that healthy eating is enjoyable, you are providing a foundation for a lifetime of healthy food habits.

## 4. EXERCISE

Exercise can be a dirty word to some people. I always hated the word because it reminded me of gym class in school. I was unathletic, uncoordinated, and the last picked for any team. The only sport I was good at was dodgeball since I didn't want to get hit by the ball!

As an adult I've discovered the joys of physical movement but the forms of exercise I do now are not traditional sports per se. I've taken swimming lessons, tai chi, aerobics, belly dancing, and yoga. These types of exercise allow me to get in touch with my body so that I don't live only in my head (this is where you only pay attention to your body from the neck up and ignore the rest of it.)

When you find the right activity, exercise doesn't feel like a chore or something to dread. Instead it feels like you are being good to your body and treating yourself with respect. Take time to find the right activity for yourself and don't be afraid to shop around to find one that fits. When you find the right one, you'll know it because it feels natural to you.

Remember not to overdo exercise, though, as that can be harmful itself. You want to feel healthier, not work your body into the ground! The endorphins that are released when you exercise make you feel great and that is a wonderful reward itself. One of the other benefits is that your daughter will see you being active and that will help her realize that physical activity is fun and that will benefit her for the rest of her life.

## 5. VOLUNTEEERING

One of the best ways to take your mind off your own issues is to help someone else in need. Volunteering is an excellent way to give something back to the community, improve your attitude, make friends, and have fun. One of the most rewarding experiences I've ever had was becoming a Big Sister to my Little Sister. We were matched for 3 1/2 years from the time she was 9 until 13. It was incredible watching her becoming strong, beautiful, and confident. I think I learned more from her than she did from me!

When you throw yourself into volunteering or other charitable causes it leaves very little time for you to mope about your appearance. You can build your confidence, learn new skills, make a difference in someone's life, and generally feel happier about making a contribution. Your daughter will also see you being charitable to others and this will make a great impression on her and help her also be kind to others.

## 6. GETTING A LIFE COACH

If you feel stuck with improving your self image and want some help with it, you may want to consider hiring a life coach. Life coaches work with you to achieve your goals faster than if you were working on them alone. A life coach will help you determine where you are in your life right now and where you want to be in the future. The coach will then help you create an action plan to achieve your goals. Your coach is your partner in the relationship but he or she will not do the work for you. These are your goals and, as such, it is your responsibility to do the work to achieve them. Of course your life coach will help you celebrate your successes and help you make adjustments to your plan if necessary.

The authors of this book are all life coaches and we all specialize in different areas. Personally, I coach teen girls in being strong, confident, and beautiful. This is my passion because I don't want anyone to grow up experiencing the pain and depression I had when I was growing up.

I have two life coaches and I can attest that both of them have helped me tremendously in my goals to become a life coach and more importantly, in my growth as a woman. I am becoming the person I was always meant to be and it is an amazing feeling to know it.

## 7. RESOURCES

What helped me the most over the past 20 years in gaining self acceptance has been reading positive, uplifting material both in print form (books and magazines) and the Internet. I've always found it helpful to find out other people's opinions and examine whether they mesh with what I believe for myself or not. For the sake of brevity, I've only listed the following resources below that I have found particularly helpful for my situation:

MAGAZINES:

**BBW Magazine** - the first one that I ever found that was geared especially for me as a larger woman (http://www.bbwmagazine.com)

**Radiance Magazine** - now defunct but back issues are still available on their website at http://www.radiancemagazine.com/

BOOKS:

These are just a few of the favourites from my bookshelves:

<u>**Life Is Not a Dress Size**</u> by Rita Farro - I love this book for the fashions and the warmth and humour of the author

<u>**Deal With It:: A Whole New Approach to Your Body, Brain and Life As A Gurl**</u> by gURL.com - excellent book for teen girls and their moms too!

<u>**Real Gorgeous: The Truth About Body and Beauty**</u> by Kaz Cooke - another awesome book for girls and their moms

<u>**Fat!So?: Because You Don't Have to Apologize For Your Size**</u> by Marilyn Wann - this is probably the most read book on my shelves. I re-read it at least every 6 months.

<u>**Real Women Don't Diet**</u> by Ken Mayer - this book tells it like it is from a man's point of view (my mother should read this book!)

<u>**Self Esteem Comes In All Sizes**</u> by Carol A. Johnson - excellent book on self esteem and how to treat yourself well no matter the weight on the scales.

**Sexy At Any Size** by Katie Arons - Katie shows us that being attractive is possible at all sizes. It all comes down to confidence!

In conclusion I'd like to say that the bond that you share with your daughter is one of the most joyful, painful, complicated relationships you will ever have. Your little girl (or big girl) is watching every move you make. She wants to grow up to be just like you. When you talk negatively about yourself or your body, she is going to pick up on that and most likely do the same to herself. You can help her immensely by learning to love yourself and show her that it is OK to love herself. By doing this for your daughter now you will ensure that future generations of women in your family will also grow up feeling happy, beautiful, and strong. What an amazing, wonderful legacy to pass on!

*Wishing you and your daughter a peaceful journey together!*
*Martyn A. Dell*

# CHAPTER NOTES

## CHAPTER SEVEN

# LOVING YOURSELF HEALTHY WHILE CREATING YOUR OWN POSITIVE BODY IMAGE

# BarBara Whorley

From an early age BarBara Whorley has had the entrepreneurial drive. Starting in the 60's, Barbara sold greeting cards out of the basket of her Schwin banana seat bike. Over the last two decades BarBara has worked in a variety of companies including a large weight loss company as a top leader and motivator being an executive recruiter, creating passion. Through the experience of starting three different companies of her own BarBara has learned the keys to building a successful company as well as the pitfalls to avoid. She has discovered that overcoming challenges and finding the right fit are paramount to success in any endeavor. Now BarBara works with bold and daring women who desire to live outside their stripes reaching for their highest goals and dreams through **Spotted Zebras of the SisterHerd Coaching**.

The Spotted Zebras of the SisterHerd was born from BarBara's own search for women like herself that desired to live outside their stripes! (Leave their comfort zone, limiting beliefs behind) The Spotted Zebras of the SisterHerd is a supportive, safe place for a woman to discover and explore her uniqueness, to celebrate who she is in her heart, mind and body. To live fully present and authentically. To Live her Life bigger than she ever believed possible. To engage passionately to reach her goals and attain every dream she DESIRES!!! A Limitless Celebration of Who she is, as a woman, in her personal life and in business. How do you become a Spotted Zebra of the SisterHerd by leaving your stripes behind... Before you know it you will be Running in the meadow of miracles, drinking from the pool of possibilities, and dancing to your inner rhythm of living your dreams, with other Spotted Zebras!!!!!!!!!!!

**BarBara Whorley**

**Mission Viejo, CA • www.spottedzebracoaching.com**

Loving yourself

Creates the elf

That can whisper to you

"This I can do."


Be a Zebra unique,

Kick up your feet,

Use your coach for all you reap,

And let  it fly!  Leap!

BarBara Whorley

# LOVING YOURSELF HEALTHY WHILE CREATING YOUR OWN POSITIVE BODY IMAGE

Imagine a little girl toddling around a play room - chubby thighs and arms, a round little Buddha belly protruding over her diaper - she is oblivious to how her body and shape compare to the other toddlers playing around her. She grins and peals with giggles at all her accomplishments, from holding a toy, to standing up, to toddling away to discover her world.

At some point this cute adorable little girl will become painfully aware of her body. At nearly every age - as a pre teen, a teenager, a young adult woman and as a full grown woman - she will learn to compare every aspect of her body to other women's bodies, most likely, not in a positive way. She will learn young how influential adults in her life view her body, as too thin, too fat, too short, too tall. They will inform her of their opinion of how she should look and what she should do about it. Without knowing it they are packing her Body Image Suit Case for a life full of negative images of herself and as worthy in society based solely by how her body looks.

Beyond the influential adults in her life, her peers and society will do a number on her, until by her teen years, she will have enough negative opinions of her body to feed a lifetime of abusive self talk and unhealthy behaviors. She will come to believe her body is not perfect as society dictates it should be.

With the message that 'looking perfect' brings complete happiness, it is no wonder eating disorders are epidemic and plastic surgery is the fastest growing type of selective surgery in America Women in other countries are not far behind in this staggering obsession to obtain the Perfect Body Image.

I lived with this message. I was the cute chubby girl who did not "lean out" at a rate that pleased the influential adults and peers in my life. I was told from a very young age that my shape was unacceptable and desperately needed to be changed. Early on I learned being gifted in school and testing well beyond my grade level would not carry as much value as becoming thin. By the time I was seven years old I sought any way possible to attain the value of being one of...'The Thin People'. Based almost entirely upon images in my mind, not what was truly reflecting back from the mirror, I acquired two eating disorders and an incredibly warped body image.

Finally, at age 30 and after birthing 4 children, I began to find the way to Love Myself Healthy while creating my own Positive Body Image.

I discovered women rarely arrived to adulthood without varying degrees of negative body image. For some it was a mild annoyance about imperfections. For others it was complete self loathing. The interesting thing was, it didn't matter what the outside wrapper looked like. The woman could be a size four to a size XXXXL. The self hate was just as intense.

While I was learning to love myself healthy, I noticed: what I loved and adored in my life, I nurtured; what I abhorred I ignored. When I abhorred my body, I gave it little care. I gave attention instead to a great hairdo or a pretty pair of shoes, yet I ignored the body in between, as if it didn't matter. I recognized whatever I attached my negative thoughts to and focused upon, expanded, be it my thighs, butt or gut! The more I complained about the body parts I hated, the more they seemed to stand out to me when I passed a mirror or tried on clothes. It was an evil plot!

My continual negative feelings around my less than perfect body kept me prisoner to constant thoughts: Why couldn't I have thighs like her? How come my stomach isn't as flat as hers? When I get pregnant, why do my baby toes gain weight too? Why didn't I lose my baby fat as fast as her? Blah blah blah... I inflicted so much torture by comparing myself to others, my brain had run a 100 mile marathon of negativity for endless days. No wonder I was too tired to exercise!

I wasn't alone in this sadistic prison. At a women's retreat, dinner with girlfriends, business seminars and public bathrooms with complete strangers, I heard them lament how unfair life was that they didn't have a perfect body. They complained, "Oh my gosh my thighs, my butt, my stomach", "I won't wear short sleeves, my arms jiggle"...

I'd heard enough, from myself and from others. "That is it! No more!" I became determined to love myself healthy while creating my own Positive Body Image - not society's version, not my family's, not men's, not other women's, but my very own Positive Body Image!

Loving myself healthy while creating my own Positive Body Image began as a quest to find freedom from the prison of "looking perfect" until it became journey of finding peace and joy in being me - Authentically ME!! - inside and out.

I share these freeing choices I have found on my own path to help you create and sustain a healthy lifestyle and your own Positive Body Image.

## SEVEN FREEING CHOICES TO LOVE YOUR SELF HEALTHY WHILE CREATING YOUR OWN POSITIVE BODY IMAGE

Develop a healthy personal eating plan for your life.

Whether it is weight loss or just to feel the best you can and get the most mileage possible from the make and model you were given, you need to find an eating plan that works for you. There are no magic pills or bullets.

I reached my goal weight, after many failed attempts with a well known weight loss company. I then worked for the company off and on since 1987 as a speaker - motivating and encouraging the members to reach their desired goal weight.

Often I observed clients embracing a program that was not a fit for their lifestyle. For a while they would white knuckle their way to achieve weight loss. Long term, they were unable to maintain their loss and would gain their weight back.

It was not until I learned to love myself healthy while creating my own Positive Body Image that I was able to easily maintain the weight loss. Only when I found an eating plan that fit my lifestyle did I achieve weight loss and maintain it easily.

Finding the plan that enhances the life you have is relatively simple. You start by acknowledging yourself and your lifestyle. Next you select a food plan you can embrace and live with, matching your basic lifestyle. When reviewing food plans, ask these questions to gain clarity on what will work to create and maintain the results you desire.

- Does this fit my lifestyle?

- Will I need to only eat their pre-packaged food?

- Are the foods ones I will eat?

- Does it offer choices I can live with?

- Can I eat out while on the program?

- Does it incorporate the healthy food guidelines i.e. grains, fruits, vegetables,  dairy, proteins and fats?

- Is it an exclusionary program that one can only do for so long then revolt with binging on a forbidden food?

In my book, there are no bad foods and eating certain foods does not make you bad. There is no "Fat Hell" people are sent to when they eat bad foods.  It is not a moral issue. Food is neutral. It's what meaning we attach to it that gives food power over us.  Bottom line when choosing a plan or program does it fit your lifestyle, does it give you the results you desire, and can you eat this way the rest of your life to maintain the results you desire?

## EAT AT TRUE HUNGER AND STOP AT COMFORTABLE

Learning to eat at true hunger and stopping at comfortable is a wonderful way to create weight loss and maintenance. Unfortunately some of us know too well the feeling of eating to what I call The Thanksgiving Dinner "Oh My Gosh I ate all that? Now I need to unbutton my pants, lie on the couch, and watch football which I hate." Syndrome.

Discovering your body's nutritional needs is paramount to creating your own Positive Body Image. Identifying what is true hunger is challenging for those whose emotional hunger for unmet needs overrides their awareness of physical hunger signals. I will address this in the 3rd choice to Loving Yourself Healthy.

For now, think of hunger on a range of 0 to 10. Zero is the feeling of starving Ten is the "Oh my gosh the turkey isn't the only one stuffed" feeling. A growling tummy to acknowledging the fact you could eat is typically at 2 or 3 on the scale.

Start to eat when your body is sending growling tummy signals. The old rule of three meals per day is not as important as learning to eat when you are hungry.

Listen for mental and physical cues of being comfortable and no longer hungry. You are not hungry when your stomach stops growling or you no longer hear the little voice in your head saying, "I am hungry."

To be able to notice, you have to check in with yourself. Try setting a timer to go off 20 minutes into dinner. Put the timer a distance away so you physically get up and go to turn the timer off. Ask yourself, "Am I still feeling hungry?"

I would set my dryer timer, which was off my kitchen. Most often I would know by then if I was comfortable and no longer hungry. Knowing what "stopping at comfortable" felt like was amazing. Before this, I would consume two In and Out™ burgers, fries and a shake in a sitting and still think I was hungry. Even now I will get up from a table at home or a restaurant to ask myself if I am still physically hungry. It keeps me from lapsing into feeding my emotions instead of physical hunger.

It is a wonderful feeling to eat to comfort instead of discomfort. When you learn your body's signals, you can learn to stop when you are comfortable but not stuffed. It seems like a small thing to do, yet learning this about yourself will lower the amount of food you tend to consume long after your body is comfortable. Just this step can create weight loss or maintenance without making changes in what you eat.

## LEARN YOUR EMOTIONAL EATING TRIGGERS

Discovering what is true hunger is a challenge when emotional hunger for unmet needs overrides physical hunger signals.

Part of learning to love yourself healthy while creating your own Positive Body Image is discovering what emotions have ownership over you and your food choices.

For the emotional eaters this will be hard to fathom but there are some individuals who have no connection with eating and emotions. If you are an not an emotional eater, keep reading. It may assist you in understanding someone you care about who is an emotional eater.

Emotional eating triggers can range from happy to the abyss of depression. For emotional eaters, food has become their comfort and their friend. They turn to food while experiencing a range of generally negative emotions.

For years I used food as my friend because food never called me names or asked me: What were you thinking? How could you do that? Why are you so stupid? Nor did food ever walk away and reject me. Not once did a bowl of ice cream go away because I wasn't attractive enough. Food never denied me, or shut me down. It was always there for me.

When I discovered I would never be fulfilled emotionally by food, and this behavior was blocking my ability to deal with challenging issues, I decided to find out what it was all about.

I began to write in my journal before eating when I knew I was feeding emotions instead of feeling them. I would write all I was feeling without censoring, scrutinizing or evaluating if it was valid or not. It didn't matter the who, what or why of the situation, just that I acknowledged my emotions.

A wonderful thing began to happen. I was eating emotionally less and less until one day I just wrote down my emotions, read them, thought of some really creative ways to deal with what I wrote...and I didn't eat a thing.

Digging for these buried feelings is important! Do this first step before doing others.

**Get a journal.** When you know, suspect or don't know if you are feeding your emotions instead of feeling them, write down all you are feeling before you eat. Censor nothing. It does not matter the who, what or why of the situation. It only matters you acknowledge and feel your emotions. When you allow yourself to feel your emotions, you the next steps may help shift the energy.

If you are experiencing anger, frustration or hurt, throw ice in the shower or bath tub or do this in the backyard if it feels better. You will have the satisfaction of something breaking, but no clean up.

Call someone who will allow you to vent and not fix you - a good friend or a coach who is working with you.

Do something for some one else. Assisting someone else is a wonderful way to move away from your self and your triggers.

## NURTURE AND TREAT YOURSELF LOVINGLY

"Treating yourself lovingly" is foreign to many women who have spent most of their lives negating themselves regarding their bodies. The constant barrage, of self loathing, thinking about what is not right with their bodies and how they find themselves unattractive, is so sad.

I have witnessed this with gatherings of friends and even in public restrooms: One woman says a negative comment about a feature of her body and in no time the entire group is competing for who has the worst butt, thighs or stomach. Women bash themselves against the rocks of society's dictation of perfection for the female body.

For fun, after coming to the place of loving my body, I would shock these women by standing there and stating how much I loved a feature on my body. I would then compliment the others about their wonderful bodies. At first they would look at me as if I had spoken a bizarre foreign language but with some encouragement, I had them asking, "What part of you do you celebrate?" and they would join in with positive affirmations about their own body.

Once when I spoke at a weekend seminar for women on Loving Yourself Healthy While Creating Your Own Positive Body Image, I asked a group of women to state three positive affirmations about each part of their body. You would have thought I had asked them to sacrifice their first born with the struggle most of them had coming up with just one positive comment.

We started with their feet and moved up their bodies. I encouraged them to daily speak affirmations regarding each part - this great gift that enabled them to do all the things they did in a day. I reminded them: Every day they are able to hug, love and achieve awesome feats with their incredible bodies.

If they were unhappy with a body part I would ask, "Is it some thing you can change with a behavior like exercise and/or modifying your eating?. Are you willing to do that?" If they were not, then I encouraged them to learn to love it, as is.

I told them my story: My thighs have always touched at the top. As a young girl I wanted what I called "pony legs", the ones you could see the sun set between. Well even when I was anorexic weighing 50 pounds less, my thighs touched at the top. Talk about a revelation! There is nothing I can do to change the fact my thighs are what you call justified to the center! They would always be that way, no matter what I weighed! I learned to love them as they were. If I choose to exercise more, they are firmer and stronger, but they will always touch at the top. So I choose to love them and be thankful I can hike, ride bikes, chase my kids, dance and get around with them.

Still, one woman in particular was beyond frustrated with the assignment when we reached the stomach. She raised her hand

"Stating there is not one positive thing about my stomach. It pooches, has ugly stretch marks and I will never have a flat stomach so I can wear a bikini again!" She asked me to give her one positive thing to say about this, as she pointed to her offending belly.

I asked her if she had children. She said yes two. "Are they healthy?" I asked. "Yes they are," she answered. I said, "If I were you, I would be thankful for the home that held my babies for the 9 months before they were born. I would be so thrilled this tummy held the most precious gifts I have ever created in my whole life. I would recognize there may be women in this room right now that would love to have a protruding stomach with stretch marks, as they will never know the feeling of giving birth."

She looked around with tears in her eyes as she realized she was thankful for her two wonderful children. The 'offensive' body part was now a badge of creation. She chose to adore and treat her self lovingly as she spoke thankful positive affirmations that day.

A few months later I received a note from her. As she made the change to speak to her body in more healthy, loving, affirming ways every day, her tummy was becoming flatter. She actually loved her stretch marks now, as they reminded her how lucky she was to give life to the two most precious gifts in her life.

When we think, speak and focus on the positive, we shift not only in perspective but also in the physical realm. What we abhor we ignore and what we adore we nurture.

I encourage you to stand before a mirror and make a list of every thing you see negative about your body.

Now I challenge you to find three positive things about that body part. From now on, state only the positive. You will be surprised how stating the positive allows you to feel positive about your body or even see physical changes.

In addition to how we see ourselves, how we give to ourselves is another aspect of nurturing and treating ourselves lovingly.

From childhood, women are taught by example to nurture others, not ourselves. How many of us have memories of our mothers cleaning house, making the meals throughout the day, driving the mom taxi, running errands, grocery shopping? Some of our moms were also working a full or part time job outside of the home.

Most of us have learned to be such givers, we don't even think about ourselves and our need for personal time. Overeaters may turn to food to ignore the need for personal time. Others of us may choose other unfulfilling activities.

In order for us to learn to nurture and treat ourselves lovingly we need to acknowledge the gap in thinking and in taking action. Some of my clients dismiss their feeling of desiring to take a few hours to themselves, let alone an entire day or two. "There is no time." they lament. Taking action means taking time for ourselves.

Think about what happens when we go 90 miles an hour meeting other's needs and not ours? At some point, resentfulness creeps in and we become generally unhappy. No longer do we derive happiness from the little things we used to enjoy. Soon everything becomes blurred by the litany of tasks and 'must dos'. Our needs as women drift so far down the list, we even forget what is important to us. We forget what speaks our very soul.

**If you are feeling dissatisfaction with your life and have lost the simple joy of being, do the following:**

- Make an list of whatever gives you joy, charges your battery and expresses to yourself that you matter. Forget how much it costs or how wild it is.

- When the list is 50 or more, categorize them.

- Earmark the simple little things

  - fresh flowers in the home or office regularly

  - read a book for fun

- create or finish an art project you may have put off forever.

- List the more time consuming and/or costly ideas, such as:

- receive regular massages

- a weekend away with girlfriends.

- see a play

- take dance or art classes

It always amazes me how so many other things in life line up, once a woman takes the time to create space in her life for herself and her desires.

Schedule it in as a priority, guard it as holy and see what happens for you. This is what feeds your very soul, something food can never accomplish! Nurture your desires, dreams and passion. These are key to learning to love yourself healthy while creating your own Positive Body Image.

## ASK FOR AND GET YOUR NEEDS MET

When you start the journey to Loving Yourself Healthy While Creating Your Own Positive Body Image, things in your life will inevitably change for the better, but it may rock other's boats. They have become accustomed to their Mom or Wife being or acting a certain way.

I remember when I decided I was going to walk daily with a friend, I asked the older children to watch the younger sibs. You would have thought I was torturing them for all of an hour. But I stuck to my guns as I needed this for my body as much as my mind at that time  After a couple months the kids noticed what the walking did for me – I was calmer and happier over all. When I hadn't taken my walk that day the kids would hand me my walking shoes and inform me I needed my walk as they too had benefited from a mom who was taking care of herself.

State what you want without making the other person wrong. Say what you need without explaining (i.e.,  well if you did this or were more this I could....)  In essence, state your wants, and if necessary, co-create a solution with the other person's assistance or support.


## CREATE A LIFE OF MOVEMENT

As mentioned above, I created movement in my life by walking with friend. For 5 years straight, we spent half the walk venting and catching up about our day, the last half was spent in prayer and creative ideas of how to deal with the issues brought up on the first half of the walk. That time in my life is very special to me. With four children under 12 at the time, it also kept me sane.

Just to clarify, I hated exercise as I was growing up. In school, PE for me stood for Physical Embarrassment. I was not good at much, I would always have a beet red face and it just wasn't fun. I would pay kids to lie for my Presidential Physical Fitness tests as I couldn't do a chin up if my life depended on it. I hated competing and always coming in last.

As an adult I discovered aerobics and weight lifting. Since they were not competitive, I thoroughly enjoyed them. I became a woman who enjoyed movement. I don't use the word exercise as it brings up too many negative connotations.

Movement can be dancing for 30 minutes to great music, walking with a friend or alone, with your thoughts or an iPod, with music or a book recorded.

Choose a movement that speaks to you and enriches you. When you embrace movement as part of your life, so many benefits come your way:

- clarity of mind

- feeling fit

- toning and firming

- longevity and many more

In the movement section of my workshops, inevitably a woman would share how she hated wearing shorts or OH MY GOSH a bathing suit in public and that is why she wouldn't do movement.

At that point I would ask "do you have children that would like to go swimming with you or play outside on a warm day". She would say yes, but she wouldn't be caught dead in shorts or a bathing suit.

I would then ask, "When your child grows up and remembers playing at a park, in the pool or at the beach, do you think they will remember what size you were or the great memory of their mom, aunt or friend playing with them?"

As women we put so many limits on our life based on our negative body image that we miss out on what I call Memory Making Opportunities to last a life time, both for ourselves and the people who love us.

## WHICH BRINGS ME TO THE 7TH CHOICE.

### *No Matter What Live Life Now!!!*

I have never been to a funeral yet where they bury a woman in her bathing suit or shorts! Nor do friends and family stand around remembering all the different sizes or weights the woman was throughout her life. Instead they speak of her heart, her laugh, her smile, her passions, her achievements, the people she loved and what she meant to them.

So women, do get over it! If you desire to lose weight, do it! Let me warn you, however, it won't be an entirely different body just a smaller version of the one you have now. Love the wonderful vehicle; the outside wrapper you are in. LIVE this life you are living!

*Love Yourself Healthy While Creating Your Own Positive Body Image Now!!! BarBara Whorley*

*CHAPTER NOTES*

## CHAPTER EIGHT

# CELEBRATING CHANGE; A GOAL ORIENTED APPROACH TO ACCEPTING CHANGES IN OUR LIFE

## Rhonda H. Smith

Rhonda H. Smith combines her experience working with small businesses and her insightfulness into the human spirit to coach women who are transitioning through changes, managing parenting issues, or advancing in their businesses, careers, or personal life.

Rhonda's clients describe her as nurturing, insightful, tactful, resourceful, thoughtful, creative, inspirational, and loyal. Her mission is nurturing and inspiring others to open new paths of self-discovery, awareness, and greatness! She is a member of the International Coach Federation and International Association of Coaches.

By working with women personally, through group coaching, tele-seminars and public speaking, Rhonda aspires to acknowledge the greatness that resides in every woman, and she encourages them to embrace their lives and celebrate the changes!

**Rhonda H. Smith**

**Orange City, FL • 978-660-9092 • www.RhondaHSmith.com**

Plan it,
Create it,
Accept it too,

Change is important
Through and through.

Harness your power
Every hour,
Go the length,
Realize your strength!

Rhonda H. Smith

## CELEBRATING CHANGE: A Goal Oriented Approach to Accepting Changes in Our Life

We go through so many changes in our lives. We grow up, we move out, we establish our own lives. Our bodies change and our minds change. We have children, we pursue education and careers. We lose relationships, loved ones, and sometimes we lose our jobs. We decide to change where we live and where we work. We grow emotionally, physcially and spiritually. Are these changes something to celebrate? Often times when we think of change, fear is our first emotion. Most people do not like to think of change, because it feels like something out of our control. When you think of change what feelings come to mind; fear, doubt, anxiety, terror, dread, the unknown, unexpected, anger? Or do you look at it with feelings of; excitement, enthusiasm, anticipation, hopefulness, eagerness, or even joy?

You have probably heard the saying, "Change is the only

constant in life." Sometimes you may feel that you are ready for all the change to stop. It won't stop, it is a constant. Since change is constantly occurring, then we must learn how to accept it, and even learn to celebrate the changes. Change is what makes life. We will have good changes, and bad changes, things we expect and things we don't expect. Change brings the opportunity to grow, learn, evolve and celebrate!

**MAJOR LIFE CHANGES**

Take a look at some of the changes we, our family, friends or acqauntances may have faced. Whatever the outcome, whether it was great joy or tremendous sadness, everyone of these events brought about change.

Look at the following chart, identify the changes that have taken place in your life:

| Graduation | Marriage | Divorce | Death |
| Break-up | Financial Gain | Job loss | Moving |
| Promotion | Financial Loss | Business | Retirement |
| Partnerships | Buying a Home | Friendships | Births |
| Dating | Career | Illness | Lawsuits |

Occasionally we may go through more than one of these changes at the same time, which truly tests our strength.

## MOTIVATIONS OF CHANGE

What motivates change?  Sometimes events happen that motivate changes, other times we seek change. Following are some stories which are depict of the motivations of changes.  All the names have been changed to ensure privacy.

### Reactionary Change

It was late Friday afternoon, around 5:20 pm, when Brenda received a call on her cell phone from her husband. "Where are you?" he asked. "Oh, I am still at work, we are working on reports the accountant needs," Brenda replied.  "Can you go home right now?" he asked, his voice sounded stressed. "I can if I need to," she answered.  "Is everything OK?" she asked.  He answered, "I can't talk about it on the phone, I will meet you at home."  Brenda quickly left work, anxious to find out what her husband wanted to talk about.  Her mind raced with possibilities; had he lost his job, had one of his parents been taken to the hospital, had their dog been injured? She went down the list of their children and when she had last spoken to each one.  To ease her anxiety she phoned her friend, Debbie, to chat during the 15 minute ride home.  She could have never expected the news she was about to receive.  Once home, her home phone rang, she answered it.  The voice on the other end of the line told her that her 17 old daughter had been found dead, apparently suicide.

This event is a perfect example of a **Reactionary Change**. This is the type of change that occurs suddenly, and therefore we must react. Other examples of reactionary change are an accident, a sudden loss of a job, illness or a divorce, events which requires us to react and realign our life.

Brenda was obviously stunned, devastated and grief stricken. But the change had occurred. From this event Brenda reports she has become an even better mother to her remaining children and now works with other parents to recognize the warning signs that come before suicide. She has taken a terrible event and brought about positive changes. She now celebrates each day she has with her children and feels she is living a more purposeful life.

## Anticipatory Change

**Anticipatory Change** is another type of change. With this type of change we have advance warning, so anticipate the effects of the change.

Ryan and Sara were anxiously awaiting the birth of their new baby. They had decorated the nursery, had a huge baby shower, and everyone in the family was excited about the arrival of the first grandchild. When Amy was born, she was quite a handful. It seemed no matter what Ryan and Sara tried, Amy cried and couldn't sleep. "This is so much more work than I expected," Sara told her mother. "Don't worry honey, it will get easier as she get a little older," her mother reassured her. Of course, Amy did get through her colic and start sleeping through the night. Even though Ryan and Sara anticipated the changes the new addition would have on their life, there were still some surprises and adjustments. Now they are a happy family and have even had another baby girl.

With **Anticipatory Change** we plan for the effects on our life. Even though we anticipate and plan, sometimes we are surprised at the effects and emotions the change brings into our life. Anticipatory changes include; retirement, getting married, moving to a new city, moving to a new home or apartment, starting a new business or new career.

**Unknown Feeling Change**

Diane always ordered a hamburger at her favorite restaurant. One day with her friend, Nancy, she decided to order a fish sandwich instead. The fish was cold and greasy. "Well, at least I tried something new," Diane happily said. "I am proud of you!" Nancy exclaimed.

This is the **Unknown Feeling Change**. With this type we may not know exactly why we want to change; we just know we want something different. Examples of this type of change maybe choosing a new place to live, trying a new route instead of the normal route, or trying something new at a favorite restaurant. This type of change allows us to explore choices and options.

Even though the experience was not great, Diane had the opportunity to explore a new option and realize that she could get out of her habits and comfort zone. Later that day at work, she decided to try a different approach with an obstinant co-worker. Fortunately, the experience was better than the 'cold fish' she had at lunch.

## Not Quite Right Change

The last type of change is **Not Quite Right Change**. With this type of change we feel that something is not quite right and that there could be something better. Stacey was unhappy in her marriage. She knew she had out grown Scott. They had gotten married when they were 20 and now at 35, she had an awesome business and was actively involved in the community. Scott, however, still had no direction or ambition. His idea of a good time was getting together with friends and partying. They had tried marriage counseling, couple's therapy, weekend retreats, and anything else Stacey could think of to bring their lives in alignment. Stacey felt in her heart that things were not quite right and that something needed to change. With the **Not Quite Right** type of change we are seeking a change for the better. Stacey and Scott did end up getting divorced. After 5 years Stacey is now happy in a new relationship. "It took me several years to rebuild my life after the divorce, even though I felt I needed the change," Stacey recently told me. Not all **Not Quite Right** types of change are this drastic, may be as simple as deciding to redecorate the house, get a new car, or just make an improvement in your health or life style.

**Areas of Change**

As we come face to face with change we realize the impact on our life. Regardless of our emotional state surrounding the change, there is an effect on our lives. We may feel a **fundamental change**, which truly changes who we are at your core, our essence. Or we may encounter a **revelatory change**, an epiphany that gives us that "a-ha" or "light bulb moment" type of change. Or we may experience a **habitual change**, where we change a long held habit, something that doesn't serve us.

**STEPS OF CHANGE**

Regardless of the type of change or the impact it has on our lives, with all change there is a process that occurs. The process doesn't necessarily happen in a specific order, but as we progress through the change we will typically experience each aspect. First we realize that the **change is occurring**, although this may take some time to recognize. Once we recognize the change is occurring, we need to **factually disengage** from the past. To do this we will need to see what the current state is, see there is a new way and accept that change is occurring. The most difficult process in change is **emotionally disengaging** from the past. We may realize there is a change but may not be accepting the change, and be yearning for 'how it used to be.' If we can see the **anticipated end** we will begin to process through the change and be on our way on the **learning curve**. This is where the opportunity begins. With each change there is the opportunity to learn and grow. Once we are completely through the change and on the other side we will **internalize the lesson,** the true blessing of change.

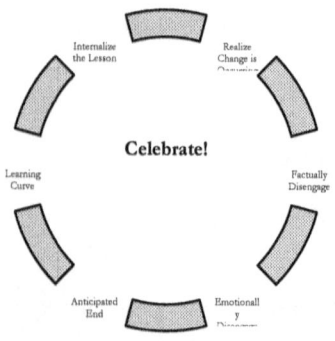

# GOAL ORIENTED APPROACH TO CELEBRATING CHANGE

There is a goal oriented approach to getting through the process of change to help you move from fear of change to acceptance and celebration. The steps are:

1. <u>Identify and define the change.</u> What is changing? What type of change is this?

2. <u>Communicate the results of the change.</u> Talk to your mate, friend, counselor or coach. Share what is changing, what type of change it is and what results you anticipate.

3. <u>Recognize what is NOT changing.</u> This is really important. It may feel as if everything is affected by the change, but take time to focus on what is not changing. This will help you adjust to what is changing.

4. <u>Remember personal greatness, strengths and qualities.</u> We may spend so much time looking at what is changing, what is not working, or what is not quite right, that we stop feeling good about ourselves. Think about your positive aspects, what you are good at, what is going right.

5. <u>Identify the positive feeling(s) the change will bring.</u> How will you grow from this change? What is the lesson? How could you help others?

6. <u>Make a new plan around the change.</u> What actions can you take?

Wat would that look like? What is the smallest thing you can do to move forward and into the energy of the change? Answering these questions will help you make a new plan around the change.

7. <u>Find a support network</u>. Depending on the type of change, you may want to hire a coach, find a support group, or hire a therapist. A support network is extremely valuable!

## POSITIVE EFFECTS OF CHANGE

Although change can be scary, and we may want to cling onto the past, there can be positive effects of change. Following are few benefits of change:

| Joy | Hope | Faith | Abundance |
|---|---|---|---|
| Love | Opportunity | Spirituality | Blessings |
| Peace | Maturity | Purpose | Wisdom |
| Enlightment | Communication | Kindness | Balance |
| Imagination | Strength | Growth | Resilence |
| Humility | Grace | Discernment | Serenity |

If we focus on the positive aspects change can bring, we will find the blessing in change, even a difficult change allow us the opportunity to grow spiritually, and may open new paths that we could have never anticipated. Change is a blessing, although most times in disguise. Learning to accept and embrace change will make it easier and may even enrich the process. The next time you face change, I encourage you to **CELEBRATE**: a new you will be emerging!

*If you are facing change and would like help through your transition please consider using a coach. Coaches are trained to help you move forward in a positive direction. Rhonda H. Smith*

*CHAPTER NOTES*

## SECTION THREE

*1 something done to amuse oneself; fun; sport; recreation*
*2 freedom or opportunity for action; scope for activity*

137

## CHAPTER NINE

# Kara Gridley

Kara is someone who knows what it's like to be living a life that is 'not quite right'. Her realization that she wasn't living 'her' life became clear when her older brother died quite suddenly at the age of 43; one thing Kara knew about her brother was that he had always lived true to himself, and this was something she had recognized and admired about him – his death spurred her to commit on a deep level to begin living more true to herself (even though at the time, she really didn't know what that meant). The only way she knew to honor and celebrate his life, was to live well herself.

Going from living 'not quite right' to something that felt right and connected to herself involved a lot of change, both inner and outer. After the commitment, over a course of years, the opportunities, events, people and information came that helped Kara create more and more a life that felt like hers. Kara now enjoys living a vibrant, fun, fulfilling, and prosperous life – in other words it feels GREAT to be living; and that's a feeling she wishes upon everyone.

Kara's particular strength is understanding the process of deep change. Not only the steps but also the perseverance to continue through change is important. Supporting people to continue once they've begun their change is her specialty; for some people beginnings are easy and follow through is not, for others the beginning is difficult – both are best helped with solid support, confidence and focus. Kara helps clients keep the big picture alive while playing with the day-to-day details and the baby steps required for change.

Kara is a poet and painter as well a coach; coaching, writing and painting all tickle her to no end, and being tickled is just plain fun.

## Kara Gridley

**Grass Valley, CA • 530-268-4777 • www.OdysseyLifeCoaching.com**

Playing brings growth
That heals the hurts,
And brings the smile to tea.

It's play don't you see
To live the true me,
With authenticity.

<u>Kara Gridley</u>

**WHAT'S THAT NAGGING FEELING?**
**TIPS FOR RE-DISCOVERING YOUR *AUTHENTIC SELF* AND FEELING JOY AGAIN IN MID-LIFE**

D
o you feel like you're in the driver's seat of your life or are you in the backseat being driven around by your life's circumstances? For some women, life has just sort of 'happened' to them, the dreams and hopes they had as young women somehow just stayed 'out there', or were put aside never to be picked up again. By mid-life there's an uncomfortable awareness of *–what*? Un-ease, something nagging…... maybe you don't have and aren't doing what you want. Perhaps relationships aren't as fulfilling as you expected they could be. Your life isn't as vibrant as you'd imagined or hoped. You realize you just don't feel joy any more. If you recognize yourself here, then read on, because life *can* be vibrant again! Sometimes we just have to do some investigating and discover what's been covering us up.

Without even knowing it we often develop roadblocks to living a life that is fun, joyous, and fulfilling – full of good times and exciting endeavors; where laughter and love are an everyday experience. These roadblocks keep us from our authentic self, the self that absolutely *loves life*. No matter what we are doing, if we are living from our authentic selves then life is fun, joyous and fulfilling. The encouraging news is that as you begin to live authentically and reclaim your dreams then you begin moving towards them. No longer being separated from yourself means you are no longer separated from your dreams, and they can begin to appear.

## WHAT IS LIVING AUTHENTICALLY?

When we look at a definition of authentic we see this:

> adj 1: conforming to fact and therefore worthy of belief; "an authentic account by an eyewitness"; "reliable information" [syn: reliable] 2: not counterfeit or copied;]

So how might this definition apply to a person? A person living the fact of who they are at core - meaning they are living from their values and desires; from their skills, talents and choices – is someone we believe. We are attracted to people in touch with and living their passion. We are energized by their quiet self-assurance, inspired by their clarity and sincerity. We feel more encouraged to *be* ourselves in the presence of someone comfortable with *being* their self. Their uniqueness awakens in us recognition of our own potential. We see them enjoying life and we want that as well.

So what gets in the way of living authentically, and thus gets in the way of feeling joy and of feeling fulfilled? What are the reasons we aren't living our unique selves? Although we could look at many aspects of this, for the purposes of this chapter I've concentrated on four areas:

- Self limiting beliefs/habits
- Caring too much about the opinion of others
- Low Self Esteem
- Lack of Self Confidence

Issues in these areas lead us to be disconnected from our true self, and can lead to that feeling of things being 'not quite right' in our world. After each section 'playwork' is presented that can get you headed in the direction of, well, yourself!

## SELF-LIMITING BELIEFS/HABITS

What are you telling yourself? Are you aware of the 'inner critic' you may be carrying around, the one that says "That'll never happen", or "You have to work hard to get ahead", "Nothing's easy for me", "Just when we get ahead financially SOMETHING happens" Sound familiar? What we tell ourselves is what colors and creates our reality. We want something, then immediately tell ourselves it won't happen…

It's like going into a restaurant, getting very excited by a delicious sounding meal and when the waiter comes to the table, looking up to say, "Oh, you're not going to bring it to me anyway are you?" and then getting up and walking away….. (leaving the waiter rather puzzled and surprised by the way!)

Pretty nuts isn't it? Yet this is what we do so often, simply because we have a belief running in our heads of what *is* or *is not* possible for us. These beliefs are 'self-limiting' because *we* limit ourselves before we even know it. But there is hope.

How do these thoughts affect your authenticity? Your attitudes and beliefs about life were learned. Your family, your community or your culture taught them. Even as well meaning as many of these lessons may have been, they don't necessarily serve YOU. Consider this - If you have a desire or dream, it's because it's in you to do, to be or to have. You simply wouldn't have it if it weren't also possible to have it or accomplish it.

So if you have thoughts or beliefs that tell you these dreams aren't possible, perhaps from an inherited belief rather than a conscious one, then you are in conflict with yourself. Being less true to yourself, less authentic, you become less than happy.

**WHAT TO DO:**

- Start by BELIEVING in your dreams, nurture a sense of excitement about them and be WILLING to allow them to come to you. To really, really allow your dreams to come try this on: BE BRAVE. Because it takes courage to change what you've always done, and particularly, what you've always thought. What if you're wrong? I would encourage you to turn it around and ask: "What if I am *right*? What if that person I imagine myself to be really *is* me?"

- Be willing to DISBELIEVE what you've always thought of yourself that doesn't feel good – try out new ideas, try on new adjectives. There are a million stories about people who made a success of themselves after many failures – what they managed to do was look ahead, keep their 'eye on the prize' and <u>believe</u>.

Believing you can achieve is everything. Being willing to look at the thoughts that stop you and say, "Yeah, but what if...?" opens up whole new worlds, and its *fun*. Think of playing, like when we were kids. In play, there is innate creativity, and things aren't taken so seriously. Shaking up your perspective in this way gets you back in the game.

**EXERCISES IN SUPPORT OF PLAYING:**

1) Spend the week noticing how you feel, and what thought preceded the feeling. Are you aware of what you're thinking? When you're feeling down, uncomfortable, angry or any number of emotions that aren't 'feeling good' – notice what is going on around you and especially what you're thinking about it.

2) Write down these thoughts you notice, just that for now, notice them and write them down. What are you discovering about yourself?

3) Ask: 'How would I feel if this wasn't what I thought?' Experience how your feeling shifts, do you feel some relief, or lightness? Do you just feel better? Less stressed? (This is from the work of Byron Katie. For further information on this process, check out her book "The Work" or her website www.thework.com)

4) Next ask, 'How would I rather feel?" Purposefully choose – how would you *like* to feel/think about the given issue or dream? (This is working with the Law of Attraction, which states, "You attract what you focus on". Further resources: Abraham-hicks at www.abraham-hicks.com and Michael Losier at www.thelawofattractionbook.com ) When you begin to identify how you'd like life to feel, and you consciously choose to feel that way, you attract more of what you want.

5) Write down the thoughts and feelings that you'd rather have, experience again how this feels for you – do you feel joy, fun,

excitement? You know you are in touch with your true self when your thought evokes a sense of feeling great.

Understanding how you think, what your thought habits are, HAS to happen for you to understand why you are where you are. These are just old habits! Not TRUTH, not the way it has to be. You learned certain ideas and created your reality from them. The good news is that with practice and commitment, you can consciously replace those thoughts with the thoughts that will support the life you want.

As you begin having more thoughts that feel good, you discover your wonderful self and your unique journey begins to unfold; suddenly you ARE living your authentic life. It may or may not involve many outward changes in your life, but it will FEEL different and if there are changes you'd like to *see* happen, it's likely they *will* happen.

## CARING TOO MUCH ABOUT THE OPINIONS OF OTHERS

Do you find yourself stifled by the fear of what other people think of you? Are you unable to move forward because there are so many you are trying to please? Are you aware of this fear?

When you are faced with a decision do you listen to your heart or are you trying to answer "What SHOULD I do?" This thought pattern stops a person cold, because you've already jumped outside yourself, to the land of 'opinion'. This can be crazy making; so much worry is present now, so much wondering 'What's right?' or wondering "What will they think of me?" It's very difficult to navigate through this. When you are boxed in by trying to figure out what someone else wants, it's very difficult to know what YOU want.

- When you are faced with a decision how do you handle it? Do you solicit advice, do you research, or do you silently worry?
- Can you identify for yourself what's going on in your process, and hear the 'inner critic' spoken of above? Are you aware of any limiting thoughts?
- Are you considering options and immediately thinking how someone else will be affected or what they may think? More importantly, does this weigh heavily in your decision making?

If you are trying to please others, if you are trying not to impact someone else or stay away from any kind of conflict then you cannot be living from your true self – instead life becomes living by fear. We, none of us, can live without impacting others. Of course we affect each other, sometimes in a way that feels good, sometimes not. No one MAKES someone else feel something however; we are all responsible for ourselves. Yet if we don't realize this then we try to make ourselves responsible (or someone else does) and then we get bound up.

If we care what other people think of us too much then we rarely know what we ourselves think, and cannot live authentically. It's like trying to be like everyone else, yet everyone is truly different. We may see likeminded-ness, may belong to groups with like purposes but ultimately we are all unique. In trying to be like everyone, we can't be anyone. Our own special light is snuffed out; we cancel out ourselves in the insane pursuit of pleasing our family, our friends, our society..... It is difficult when someone is displeased, but if fear of their displeasure guides your choices then your true self has no expression, and this affects how we feel about ourselves and about life in general.

**WHAT TO DO:**

- With grace and integrity stand up for what you want. Be purposeful, be responsible and say 'THIS is what I want' and accept how others react. It is so simple in one way and profoundly difficult if you haven't lived that way. Standing firm, while allowing others their opinions, reactions and expressions involves courage. Avoiding unpleasant reactions by ignoring your desires becomes a detriment to your spirit. The choice as with everything is yours.

- In time, when living from your choice and less by what others think, you will likely find that people don't react so badly after all. Our worries are so often unfounded! Suddenly a world of freedom opens up. Your heart opens up, you are liberated from fear and you feel enthusiasm and eagerness. You want to share that joy with others and life holds a new spark.... What a wonderful world indeed!

- Care more about how you feel rather than what other people think of you. When you catch yourself say "Oh yeah, I forgot, there's that old habit." Give yourself a thumb's up when you express yourself truthfully.

**EXERCISE IN SUPPORT OF PLAYING:**

1) This will take some time, give it a few days, or weeks:
   a. Again, keep track, notice when faced with a decision, and feeling uncomfortable, what is behind it?
   b. Inside, are you thinking about how you will appear to others? Or how they will react? Note what is going on.

2) When you consider your list ask:

    a. "What is the worse thing that could happen"? Let yourself imagine just what is behind the fear – just what is it you don't want someone to think about you?

    b. Those things you don't want someone to think – a) are they true of you? (are you really selfish, or a pig, or not smart etc. etc) Give yourself the benefit of the doubt!   b) Is it even important if they think that?

3) With some things you can help yourself get past the worry by simply asking the person directly, 'Is this what you think?' The answer may be yes, yet the question dispels the energy of it. It just may not be that important, even if they do think something negative about you. Living your life in a way that feels good to you becomes the priority when you decide to live true to yourself.

4) If you're worrying about something general like, "people" will think this… really consider how much you want to live this way. There will ALWAYS be people who like what you do, and those that don't. Can you decide today to live by <u>your</u> values and wishes?

Most of the things we avoid doing to please other people are not big deals yet we've let them become so. There was a time I even dressed thinking about who I was going to see and wondering if they'd like it, or if they'd wear it! What tyranny is that? This was a tyranny I allowed to ruin even the simple pleasure of dressing to please myself. This seemingly silly habit caused daily stress. When I began to be aware of it, I decided I didn't want to care that much what other people thought of me, because it made me not be *me*.

## LOW SELF ESTEEM

Do you value your accomplishments, or are you always looking at what you didn't manage to do?  Do you constantly compare yourself to others and come up short? Have you focused so long on every mistake you've ever made, in every area of your life, that now you have a constant feeling of never getting it right or being enough?

❖ **Other signs of low self-esteem:**
- Regular feelings of being victimized
- Frequent criticism of others or circumstance
- Constantly apologizing to others
- Denigrating yourself
- Frequent regrets about the past

- Engaging in regular self-sabotage (addictions, abuse etc)

One can feel how much energy it takes up to feel bad about yourself when you look at the list above. It's so much about the past and the emphasis is on what is wrong. There is so little positive creation going on. There's no room for celebration.

When we do not celebrate our accomplishments, we do not carry hope for ourselves or for our lives and therefore we often don't give our desires their due – we don't feel worthy of them after all.

So what is true of you? Do you feel you are born worthy and valued in this world? Do you express the innate gifts that you have? Are you distracted from your authenticity and therefore your joy by the unresolved issues of your past and the misplaced beliefs about yourself? Let's look at some ways to raise ones' self esteem.

## WHAT TO DO:

- Begin looking at what is right about yourself and about your life. If this is a hard stretch for you, below is an exercise that will help you recognize what is working around you and reveals what is already right inside of you.

- Realize you see in others what is in you as well. You can use this to raise your self-esteem and feel better. As you do, you begin living more authentically.

**EXERCISE IN SUPPORT OF PLAYING:**

1. Spend time each day observing people you interact with, with the express purpose of noticing what you like about them. What are the qualities they have that you like or enjoy? What do they do that you admire and why? Keep a list of these things.

   o The qualities you notice actually reveal what IS inside you – because you simply don't respond to something in someone else that isn't in you as well – it's the Law of Attraction, like attracts like.

   For example: Is someone particularly giving and you always noticed that? If in the past you felt you weren't particularly giving, this brings hope – because the potential for giving IS part of who you are.

   Allow yourself to feel this and notice how your actions change over time. You may notice that giving comes more easily to you, that it's more spontaneous and fun – this authentic part of yourself gets expressed, you feel lighter, more fun, happier – you are living, and appreciating, who you are.

2. Next spend a week where every day you list what you do well. EVERY day come up with something you do or have done well.

No thinking about anything else. This may take some practice, but the more you begin to notice, the more you WILL notice. You have incredible qualities, talents and skills that are being overlooked- that's all; they've been dismissed, un-celebrated. In other words the focus was on what wasn't right about you instead of what *is* right. It takes practice to develop self-talk and grow self-esteem!

o   Consider having a friend help you with this. Tell them you want help changing how you view yourself. Ask them what they see in you- and let yourself hear them.

o   Tell them what you see in yourself that you like – it may feel awkward at first and that's okay – you'll begin to <u>like</u> liking yourself. It is fun to feel lighter about ourselves and want to treat ourselves well – the natural empowerment this brings opens worlds of possibility.

## LACK OF CONFIDENCE

Does everything feel 'iffy' to you? Your life, the future, how you'll manage, what you're doing and where you're going? If self-doubt is something you live with every day, where you question every step you take and always feel scared, than you are experiencing a basic lack of self-confidence. And another important question is: Do you know yourself? Do you know what you value and see how you live those values?

A lack of self-confidence directly affects living authentically; if you are not confident in your 'self', you aren't likely to be living *who* you really are. Confidence is what allows us to take risks, try new things, and go against the crowd. It's what helps us feel calm in moments when we're alone, makes it possible for us to relax in the world. When you lack self-confidence there are so many places where <u>you</u> are stopped – you don't say what you need or want to say, you don't do what you need or want to do, you doubt your abilities and feel bad about yourself.

Usually lack of confidence also includes lack of self-esteem, although not the other way around. There are many very confident people who actually possess low self esteem, which shows itself in many ways – lack of self care, abuse, unhealthy habits or self sabotage.

Often we have a lack of confidence about certain areas of our life, not in all of them. Those places where we don't feel confident can color our whole life. What we don't feel confident about haunts us until we focus more on the lack than where we feel good, or strong about ourselves.

Those dominant thoughts hold power over us because we focus on a perceived lack. Without examining this, and digging ourselves out from under low self-confidence, our authenticity suffers. We hide and whenever you are hiding your true self cannot be revealed.

**EXERCISE IN SUPPORT OF PLAYING:**

1. Affirm to yourself: I make the best decisions for myself at any given time.

- Focus on an area of your life that you do have confidence about, really FEEL what that is, what is the essence of that confident feeling? Soak it in and become familiar with it.

- Ask "what if I felt this way regarding X, what would that be like? This is the opposite of imagining the worse case scenario, instead imagine the *best* case scenario! This is the What If- UP game created by Eva Gregory and Jeanna Gabellini – it puts you in the space of possibility and let's you feel what it is you want to feel. Imagine bringing the confident feeling into an area where you are lacking it.

2. What are your strengths? We all have strengths and yet often we overlook them. Begin to notice and list your strengths, ALL of them. Are you a fantastic baker? Are you a great friend? Do you finish things? Are you creative? Are you organized? Are you a problem solver? Are you patient? Persuasive? Punctual? If we begin to know what our strengths are we can bring them into any activity and gain confidence as we go.

It *is* possible to raise our self-confidence and self esteem. When we feel better about ourselves we're more likely to be willing to go after what we want in life. We are more apt to let our unique interests, talents and values be expressed; we experience more freedom and joy.

**SUMMING UP:**

The areas and exercises we've looked at here:

- Realizing our self limiting beliefs/habits and changing them to be supportive of ourselves
- Choosing to care about our own opinions and desires more than other people's
- Raising our self esteem and self confidence;

all lead to our feeling back in the driver's seat of our own lives.

If you've been feeling uninspired and as though your life has no joy or purpose anymore, it's time to evaluate where you are. Recognizing what may be blocking your authentic self gives you the opportunity to change. You can change direction at <u>any</u> time. Right now, in this red-hot minute, you can begin to move towards more joy, fun, fulfillment, peace, prosperity – whatever it is you want more of.

Make the decision and choose to let go of what is keeping you from you. With love and practice you can change habits that don't serve you. Developing a support network is key: hire a coach, make a pact with a friend, find a group – anyone who can act as your witness, be your advocate, cheer you on and remind you how well you're doing. Be gentle and patient with yourself on this path, you've lived a long time in a certain way and it will take time to develop these valuable habits of thought and action.

Living from your true self is naturally fun, and it serves a larger purpose too – *living an authentic life encourages others to do so as well.* Be the light that helps others shine. Never give up on your dreams or yourself, and enjoy the ride!

*Kara Gridley*

*CHAPTER NOTES*

## CHAPTER TEN

## Arty laughter

# Donna Colter

Donna Colter, **Queen of Laughter** has a background in Nursing, the garment industry, and teaching. Her eclectic life experiences have provided a great foundation for learning how to laugh. Donna has one of the biggest hearts in the country and thus, is a laughter coach with compassion for the client, remedies for the serious, and humour for the courageous steps ahead. Her recent work has taken her to learning how money grows, and laughing all the way to the bank!

### Donna Colter

Calgary, Alberta •403-285-6596•www.ReachTheTopCoaching.com

Laugh with intention,
And please don't mention
The grumpy part of life,

The hard stuff gets done
When we make it fun,
A Coach is the one!

Donna Colter

# Arty Laughter

Art is an amazing part of every culture. Art stimulates imagination and creativity, dreams and desires, and new ideas. Art recalls the memories of time, place, emotions, and experiences that center around people, places, concepts and things.

Laughter is an Art form! There are giggles and guffaws, smiles and snickers, titters and tickles, belly laughs and baritone rumbles, plus the whole musical score from base to shriek. Laughter in its many forms of expression also stimulates creativity, action, passion and energy. We may laugh because of what we see, hear, or feel, and we may need to learn to laugh because of what we don't see, hear, or feel.

What does learning to laugh really mean? Isn't something funny or not? With life and all its responsibilities, when are we going to laugh? What in fact, do we have to laugh about?

The reality of life is that we design our own life and each day within it. We design the pattern of our life quite easily. We determine when we get up, brush our teeth, comb our hair, and get dressed. We design the order of these events, their timing, how we do it, and how and when we complete it. We make the choices at some point to create this part of our experience within our day. We change why and how and when we do these routines to suit our needs best.

See how we design routines into our lives? Well, we can also design laughter into our life! Children laugh hundreds of times in a day for the sheer joy of the energy of living! Adults laugh only a few times a day because something has happened to their energy as well as their joy of living. Don't we all need to laugh more? Let's get creative.

We can design when we laugh, why we laugh, if we laugh, and how we laugh. The "who of laughing is you – and if you laugh around others, chances are they will laugh too. Being the creators of our day, we can control laughter in such good ways to enrich many experiences and times in our lives. You may think you don't control your laughter but you do control you attitude regarding laughter. The attitude of "it's okay to laugh when this or that happens", "when this point in time comes or goes" or the attitude of "I can face the attention laughing brings to me right now". We all chose what we think is funny and what we'll allow ourselves to laugh about just like we chose if we'll laugh at the same joke we've heard before.

We may feel that we have created our experiences in life by default – just drifting along, fitting in, and living life vicariously through others. The result is we feel down and out and we project more negativity to others. We are not winners or losers in this life, we are choosers! Choose how you are going to live. Living life by default is a choice: We can choose to live life that way and we can choose to live life in other ways also so why not choose to live life happy? Choosing to add laughter will ensure we have a more positive, energetic, and upbeat life.

As adults, we have all made decisions why we laugh which often reflect our level of self-esteem. The decision of why we don't or won't laugh often stems from morals and standards of humour such as not liking black humour, hurtful humour veiled humour, or sarcasm. If we choose not to laugh at others, it doesn't mean we shouldn't laugh, it just means we made a choice of where not to laugh.

Create some laughter into your day. Sing in the shower, laugh in the shower, smile at yourself in the mirror. Smile at every red light you stop at on the way to work! Instead of telling your family to have a good day, teach them to laugh and have a happy day. It will help them in any situation that arises. Wear some happy clothes – clothes that make you feel good. Conscientiously laugh before you get up in the morning! (pssst! this will get your partners attention real fast!)

Learn these two exercises to get started elevating your day and increasing your energy level.

1.   Pretend you have a straw balanced horizontally between your lips only – make the corners of your lips reach to your ear lobes! It may be difficult to believe right now that frowning uses more muscles than smiling.  The strain you're experiencing right now will disappear with a little practice.

2.  Using the words Ho Ho Ha Ha Ha, repeat them in rhythm while you exercise.  You can accommodate the rhythm of this chant with walking, rowing, bending, lifting, or swinging your arms.  If you're just sitting in a chair, lift your feet off the floor and laugh – Ho Ho Ha Ha Ha.

The magic of laughing is that your brain doesn't know whether there is humour involved or not.  When you laugh with intention like this, your brain will still release those feel good endorphin hormones.  You will still enjoy the benefits of less value on your stress-o-meter, more concentration power, more energy, and a happier more positive day.  Fake it and you will make it!

Go ahead and be creative.  Plan your day and create some laughter to color your day happy.

*Donna Colter*

*CHAPTER NOTES*

# In Her Power

**In Her Power**

She takes the time to listen in the Silence

Hearing the inspired voice within

**In Her Power**

She knows that she must first cherish Herself

That all doing for others will flow from Self-Love

**In Her power**

She recognizes that time for herself is a priority, a necessity

Rather than a luxury

**In Her Power**

She laughs a deep, belly laugh

Creating a world of joyful living around her

**In Her Power**

She draws all the resources to herself

That she needs for her journey

**In Her Power**

She affirms her Worth daily by

Consciously choosing thoughts of Love every moment

**In Her Power**

She is unstoppable, passionate as she moves towards her dreams –

Nothing seems too grand for her to accomplish

**In Her Power**

She trusts her intuition, listening and

Receiving guidance for her journey

 **In Her Power**

She feels every emotion on the human scale,

Celebrating life's complexities

 **In Her Power**

She sits with her fear

Knowing it can't overcome her

 **In Her Power**

She recognizes the Goddess within and

Helping others to see their own inner Goddess

 **In Her Power**

She easily glides through life circumstances

Singing her inspired melody

For there is nothing and no one that can shake her

When she is fully, completely, peacefully

**In Her Power**

*© Patricia G. Omoqui 2006, All Rights Reserved*

Patricia Omoqui is an inspirational speaker, writer, life coach and humanitarian. Her work inspires people to achieve their dreams and reach their full life potential. www.patriciaomoqui.com